A Hedonist's guide to
Istanbul

BY Nick Hackworth
PHOTOGRAPHY Nick Hackworth

A Hedonist's guide to Istanbul

Managing director – Tremayne Carew Pole
Marketing director – Sara Townsend
Editor – Susannah Wight
Maps – Richard Hale
Design – P&M Design
Typesetting – Dorchester Typesetting
Repro – PDQ Digital Media Solutions
Printed in Italy by Printer Trento srl

Publisher – Filmer Ltd
Additional photography - Selim Sahin, Turkish Culture & Tourism Office

With thanks to Mehmet Eskihancilar and Hila @ Quintessentially
Istanbul, November Paynter, Varsif Kortun, Dephne Koryurek, Emre
Mengu, Volkan Casir, Attiye and Hakka Gokmen and Brian Sewell.

Email – info@ahedonistsguideto.com
Website – www.ahedonistsguideto.com

First published in the United Kingdom in October 2005 by
Filmer Ltd
47 Filmer Road
London SW6 7JJ

ISBN – 1–905428–00–6

Hg2 Istanbul

CONTENTS

How to…

A Hedonist's guide to… is broken down into easy to use sections: Sleep, Eat, Drink, Snack, Party, Culture, Shop, Play and Info. In each of these sections you will find detailed reviews and photographs.

At the front of the book you will find an introduction to the city and an overview map, followed by descriptions of the four main areas and more detailed maps. On each of these maps you will see the places that we have reviewed, laid out by section, highlighted on the map with a symbol and a number. To find out about a particular place, simply turn to the relevant section, where all entries are listed alphabetically.

Alternatively, browse through a specific section (e.g. Eat) until you find a restaurant that you like the look of. Next to your choice will be a small coloured dot – each colour refers to a particular area of the city – then simply turn to the relevant map to discover the location.

Updates

Owing to the lengthy publishing process and shelf life of books it is very difficult to keep travel guides up to date – new restaurants, bars and hotels open up all the time, while others simply fade away or just go out of style. What we can offer you are free updates – simply log on to our website www.ahedonistsguideto.com or www.hg2.net and enter your details, answer a question to provide proof of purchase and you will be entitled to free updates for a year from the date that you sign up. This will enable you to have all the relevant information at your fingertips whenever you go away.

In order to help us, if you have any comments or recommendations that you would like to see in the guide in future please feel free to email us at info@ahedonistsguideto.com.

The concept

A Hedonist's guide to… is designed to appeal to a more urbane and stylish traveller. The kind of traveller who is interested in gourmet food, elegant hotels and seriously chic bars – the traveller who feels the need to explore, shop and pamper themselves away from the madding crowd.

Our aim is to give you the inside knowledge of the city, to make you feel like a well-heeled, sophisticated local and to take you to the most fashionable places in town to rub shoulders with the local glitterati.

In today's world work rules our life, weekends away are few and far between, and when we do go away we want to have the most fun and relaxation possible with the minimum of stress. This guide is all about maximizing time. Everywhere is photographed, so before you go you know exactly what you are getting into; choose a restaurant or bar that suits you and your demands.

We pride ourselves on our independence and our integrity. We eat in all the restaurants, drink in all the bars and go wild in the nightclubs – all totally incognito. We charge no one for the privilege of appearing in the guide; every place is reviewed and included at our discretion.

We feel cities are best enjoyed by soaking up the atmosphere and the vibrancy; wander the streets, indulge in some retail relaxation therapy, re-energize yourself with a massage and then get ready to eat like a king and party hard on the stylish local scene.

We feel that it is important for you to explore a city on your own terms, and while the places reviewed provide definitive coverage in our eyes, one's individuality can never be wholly accounted for. Sometimes if you take that little extra time to wander off our path, then you may just find that truly hidden gem that we missed.

Istanbul

For much of human history it has been the greatest city on earth. Byzantium, Constantinople, Istanbul – the names by which the city has been known during its 28 centuries of existence are alone enough to conjure such a wealth of legends and stories as to stupefy the most curious. In that time it played various cameo roles in the great sweeps of ancient history before moving centre stage as the capital of, successively, two of the world's most powerful empires. Between Constantine's redefinition of the city in AD 330 as the New Rome and the final wreck of the Ottoman Empire in World War I, 97 Latin and Byzantine emperors and empresses and 30 Ottoman sultans ruled their lands from within its walls.

Rumours of the city's splendours, which exhausted the superlatives of the most flowery of high Ottoman poets ('Stambul, peerless of cities, thou jewel beyond compare') have always attracted outsiders. Some came without invitation – the city was seriously besieged 22 times by assorted Greeks, Romans, Franks, Persians, Avars, Slavs, Arabs and Turks. Others, drawn to its centre from the vast imperial peripheries, settled to create the world's first truly cosmopolitan city. For adventurous Europeans from Lord Byron to Pierre Loti, meanwhile, the place was a summation of the exotic attractions of the Orient. For them, like Venice, it was a city to be approached by water from which vantage could be seen, if the timing was right, an otherworldly silhouette of minarets and domes set against a chromatic sunset.

Though the flow of visitors never ceased, the last century was not kind to Istanbul, and the City of Cities faded a little from the world's collective memory. But now there are serious signs of revival. The city has quadrupled in size over the last few decades as Anatolians have migrated westward in search of betterment in the big city. Of more interest to the visitor, however, will be the hip, contemporary edge that a new generation of young, wealthy Istanbulus have conjured. Slick restaurants replete with asymmetric lighting displays and cool serving staff serve up new-fangled fusions such as beef carpaccios on a bed of pak choi while round the corner home-grown classics such as *hunkar begendi* are made with ingrained expertise in eateries that flourished while the sultans still ruled. Meanwhile dance acts from Stockholm or Berlin play to heaving crowds in clubs next door to venues playing Turkish folk.

In what is a hallmark of the greatest cities, Istanbul offers a vibrant present set within a captivating past and visitors are advised to neglect neither.

A few last words by way of introduction – get (mildly) lost (walking). In such a large and, at times, chaotic city, a guide-book, such as this one, should prove invaluable. But if you're unfamiliar with the city, clear a day, head for the middle of the Old City Sultanahmet, put away your maps and guidebooks and wander. After one such walk, though history does not record whether he got lost or not, Lord Byron wrote: 'I have seen the ruins of Athens, of Ephesus, and Delphi. I have traversed great part of Turkey, and many other parts of Europe, and some of Asia; but I never beheld a work of nature or art, which yielded an impression like the prospect on each side from the Seven Towers to the end of the Golden Horn.'

CULTURE

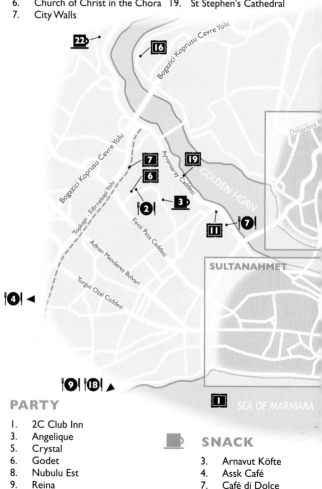

PARTY

SNACK

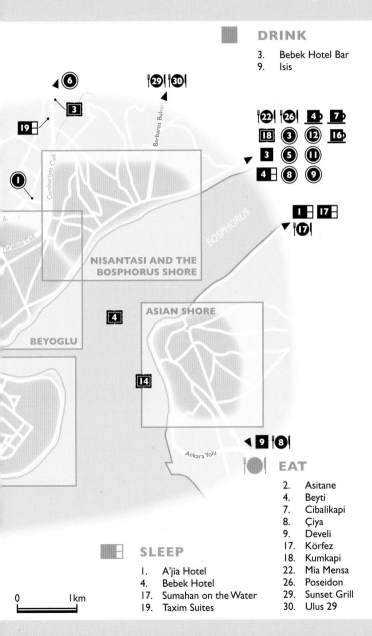

Istanbul city map

DRINK

3. Bebek Hotel Bar
9. Isis

NISANTASI AND THE BOSPHORUS SHORE

ASIAN SHORE

BEYOGLU

Cumhuriyet Cad

Tarlabasi Cad

Barbaros Bulvarı

BOSPHORUS

Ankara Yolu

0   1km

EAT

2. Asitane
4. Beyti
7. Cibalikapi
8. Çiya
9. Develi
17. Körfez
18. Kumkapi
22. Mia Mensa
26. Poseidon
29. Sunset Grill
30. Ulus 29

SLEEP

1. A'jia Hotel
4. Bebek Hotel
17. Sumahan on the Water
19. Taxim Suites

Sultanahmet

This is the ancient city, a spit of land bounded by water to the north, south and east, and to the west by the walls built by Theodosius II in the 5th century. Now a ruined and largely forgotten series of punctuation marks in the city's landscape, they protected the Byzantines for a thousand years until, in 1453, Mehmet the Conqueror breached the walls and claimed it as the capital of the Ottoman Empire.

There are few places in the world where the relics of history are more concentrated or more astonishing than within this circumscribed area. Accordingly a tourist trail centuries old connects its great mosques, museums, bazaars and palaces. Disdain for conventional sightseeing aside, they are a must.

Most are to be found in the Sultanahmet area, the eastern portion of the old city. Supremely famous, and lying at its heart, is the Hagia Sophia, Church of Divine Wisdom, for a millennium the largest building on earth. Its vast, apparently miraculously unsupported dome and spacious interior profoundly impressed Ottoman architects who answered with the Sultanahmet Mosque (also known as the Blue Mosque), its immediate neighbour, and the great Süleymaniye Mosque, which lies a kilometre away to the northwest. Together the three buildings dominate the spectacular skyline. Less vertical, but no less

impressive, the Topkapı, palace of sultans for some 400 years and byword for the mystique and baroque splendour of Oriental majesty, sits on a promontory overlooking the confluence of the Golden Horn and the Bosphorus. Its secrets and treasures are now offered up for global consumption. Delicately ornamented helmets and shields, and jewel-encrusted daggers and chests full of gemstones fill spotlit cases in the Treasury, while a reasonably priced ticket grants admission to the Harem, where once only few could enter without fearing death.

Added to this are museums of archaeology, mosaics and Islamic arts,

the ruins of the Hippodrome, obelisks and columns, cisterns and aqueducts, jewel-like churches and elegant mosques, all combining to create a fantasy-like world, steeped in the past.

Successfully puncturing those dreamlike reveries, however, are the usual tourism-spawned irritations of naff cafés, tourist-tat touts and sleazy salesmen that infest the Sultanahmet area and that other great tourist magnet that lies to its west, the Kapalı Carşhi, or Grand Bazaar. But this is an essential Istanbul experience, and visitors can be comforted in the knowledge that locals as well tourists throng its myriad streets in search of a bargain or two.

The effects of the tourist trade also mean that, perversely, unlike the rest of Istanbul, there are only a handful of good restaurants in the area and even fewer drinking or partying spots, confirming the old city as primarily a zone of cultural attractions. But when they are this splendid only the churlish would complain.

CULTURE

Cobblestone
Soğukçeşme
Sokaqi

SLEEP

SHOP

Sultanahmet local map

0   250   500m

GOLDEN HORN

Kennedy Caddesi

Ankara Caddessi

Hudavendigar Cad.

Ebusuud Caddesi

endi Cad.

Ankara Cad.

Kennedy Caddesi

2

25

Babi Ali Caddesi

27 **12** **24** **3**

18 Alemdar Cad. **12**

Divan Yolu Cad.

23 **15** **10** **28** **8**

23 **16**

11 **21** **10**

17 **20**

Uçler Sk.

Küçük Ayasofya C. **18**

9 **1** **3**

ya-Sirkeci Sahil Yolu

Beyoğlu

Beyoğlu has always been the racier, modern and outré counterpart to the fading, stately and traditional grandeur of Sultanahmet. The area of Galata, just over the Goldern Horn, was even in the days of Byzantium the home of foreign workers and merchants. On Galata Bridge the celebrated 19th-century Italian travel writer Edmondo de Amicis observed the parade of people who made up the Ottoman world – Albanians, Armenians, Africans, Jews, Tartars and Turks – and called them 'a changing mosaic of races and religions, that is composed and scattered continually with a rapidity that the eye can scarcely follow'.

In late Ottoman times the area of Pera, north of Galata, took shape, where ambitious Europeans set up hotels, notably the Pera Palace, and embassies such as Charles Barry's neoclassical British Consulate. It was here that electricity, telephony and the general trappings of modernity crash-landed into the hidebound Ottoman world. Their allure proved irresistible and in the mid-19th century the sultans implicitly acknowledged the shift of power, abandoned the Topkapı and built a succession of palaces along the nearby Bosphorus shore. Beyoğlu's great artery, the Grand Rue de Pera (renamed İstiklal Caddesi in the early days of the Turkish Republic), was then a parade of European culture and manners, while in the backstreets a more louche and bohemian atmosphere reigned, fuelled by a concoction of artists, dancers, prostitutes, pimps, writers and spies. When people wax lyrical about the cosmopolitan charms of old Constantinople, it is late-19th-century and early to mid-20th-century Pera that is in the   forefront of their minds, with the melancholy relics of Old Stamboul forming a picturesque backdrop.

The area retained that character till the 1950s, when an upsurge in Turkish nationalism convinced most minorities to leave. That's now distant history and although Beyoğlu will never again be home to such a kaleidoscope of nations, it has reclaimed its buzz. İstiklal Caddesi is high-street hideousness writ large, the beautiful 19th-century façades of its buildings hidden by hoardings and neon lights. Off its length, however, run streets that are home to innumerable and wonderful cafés, bars, restaurants, music venues and clubs, many open till the early hours of the morning.

Azmalımescit, westwards off the bottom end of İstiklal, is a particular hotspot that has benefited from artist-led gentrification, with some of the best restaurants in town sitting beside a selection of cool bars and the city's top dance and music club, Babylon, round the corner. Similarly the neighbouring areas of Çukurcuma and
Cihangir, on the other side of İstiklal, are riding high on a property price boom, thanks to the creative types who have brought them credibility. Here the bars and restaurants are particularly fashionable, nodal points of an exclusive local social scene.

Further north up İstiklal, Çiçek Pasajı, one of the many attractive passages that run off the main thoroughfare, is filled with smart waiters dying to tempt you into their admittedly charmingly appointed restaurants. Better, however, to avoid their touristy slickness and turn the corner to experience the rough and ready attractions of the fish market and its adjacent stretch of *meyhanes* (taverns), Nevizade Sokak, both overflowing with the exuberant energy of street life.

At its northern conclusion İstiklal finally empties out into the large and largely unappealing expanse of Taksim Square, a suitably symbolic separation, perhaps, between the many joys of Beyoğlu and the business district beyond.

DRINK

1. 5 Kat
2. Badehane
4. Beyoglu Pub
5. Büyük Londra Hotel Bar
6. Dulcinea
7. Galata Bridge Bars
8. Gizil Bahçe
10. The James Joyce
11. K.V.
12. Kays
13. Kino
14. Leb-i-Derya
15. Nu Terras
16. Pia
17. Soho Terras
20. Urban

SNACK

1. Alti Café
5. Bambi
8. Carnival
11. House Café
12. Kaffeehaus
13. Leyla
14. Limonlu Bahçe
17. Markiz Café
19. Miss Pizza
20. Nature and Peace
21. Pera Palace
24. Simdi
25. Smyrna
26. Sugar Club Café
28. Tapas Bar

PARTY

2. 360°
4. Babylon
7. Nu Club
10. Safran
13. Zarifi
14. Mojo
15. Nardis Jazz Club
16. Roxy

SLEEP

2. Ansen Suite Hotel
6. Büyük Londra Hotel
13. Marmara Istanbul
14. Marmara Pera
15. Pera Palace
16. Richmond Hotel

SHOP

Faik Paşa Yokuşu
Istiklal Caddesi

0 250 500m

EAT

1. 360°
6. Changa
10. Doga Balik
12. Flamm
13. Galata Bridge Fish Grills
14. Galata House
15. Haci Abdullah
20. Lokal
21. Lokanta
23. Nevizade Sokak
27. Refik
32. Wanna
33. Yakup 2

CULTURE

9. Galata Mevelevihanesi
10. Galata Tower
27. Kallavi 20
28. Ial
29. Kazablanka

Nişantaşı and the Bosphorus Shore

North and northeast of Beyoğlu lie the lands of Istanbul's haute bourgeoisie and the playgrounds of the super-rich. The inland area of Nişantaşı comprises smart streets of modern apartment blocks, fashion boutiques, good restaurants and people-watching cafés. It doesn't attract too many visitors, who tend to have homegrown versions of the Bosphorus Shore, but it's worth seeing to form a holistic impression of the city, which isn't just about fading historical relics. The Beyman Brasserie in the Beyman department store on Abdi Ipekci Caddesi, a leafier and more genteel take on Bond Street, is an excellent point from which to get the measure of the area. From there you can saunter in and out of the usual slew of designer operations – Gucci, Vuitton, Burberry and so on – before refreshing yourself at top restaurants such as Loft or Borsa. In short, Nişantaşı is a showcase for sleek, modern Istanbul.

The Bosphorus, stretching 14 miles from the Sea of Marmara to the mouth of the Black Sea, is rather more timeless. Its name is mythical: Zeus seduced Io, and so his wife, Hera, took revenge by turning Io into a heifer incessantly tormented by a gadfly. To escape the midge she swam the straits, hence 'Bosphorus' – 'ford of the ox'. Its treacherous currents, which run north–south and vice-versa (driven by differing water pressures if you must know), are immortalized in the legend of Jason and the Argonauts who famously navigated the channel's vicious, clashing rocks. But anyone who takes a recommended Bosphorus cruise (see Culture) will marvel more at the Greek gift for exaggeration than the danger, since the rocks quite clearly do not move.

More recently the Bosphorus has been the fantastical playground of the city's elite. It was here that the sultans moved after abandoning the

Topkapı, building first the rather tasteless rococo pile that is the Dolmabahçe, the Çırağan Palace, the Beylerbeyi Palace (on the Asian shore) and, finally, Yıldız Palace, which sits on a hillside of lovely woods, ponds and streams, just over the road from the Çırağan. Their wealthy subjects meanwhile studded the shoreline all the way up to the Black Sea with their *yalıs* (wooden summer mansions), still some of the world's most desirable properties.

Despite, presumably, possessing neither palace nor *yalı*, you can enjoy the Bosphorus at any of the excellent cafés, clubs and restaurants as you journey northwards along its shore. The area of Oratköy, with its Italian-style piazza, is a trendy hotspot, just past the kilometre-long Atatürk bridge. Kuruçeşme is home to super-clubs Rainer, Sortie and Angelique, as well the trendy Aşşk Café and Italian restaurant Mia Mensa. Further along, Bebek, the loveliest of the Bosphorus villages, as they were before being encompassed by Greater Istanbul, boasts the renowned fish restaurant Poseidon, a fabulous bar at the back of the stylish Bebek Hotel, and Meşhur Bebek Badem Ezmesci purveyors of what may be the finest *badem ezmesci* (marzipan) in the world.

Round the next bend stand icons of antiquity and modernity: the imposing Ottoman castle, Rumeli Hisarı (and on the opposite shore its twin Anadolu Hisarı), and the Fatih Mehmet Bridge, a world-beating suspension bridge linking Europe to Asia. Funnily enough, it's sited exactly where King Darius of Persia built a pontoon bridge in 512 BC so he could attack the Scythians. Just another place where the city's present is in play with its past.

Nişantaşı and the Bosphorus local map

BOSPHORUS

0   250   500m

SHOP
- Abdi Ipecki Caddesi

CULTURE
8.   Dolmabahçe Palace
25. Istanbul Modern
26. Atatürk Cultural Centre

SNACK
2.   Armani Caffe
6.   Beyman Brasserie

EAT
5.   Borsa
11. Feriye
19. Loft
24. Nis
31. Vogue

SLEEP
5.   Bentley Hotel
7.   Çiragan Palace
18. Swissôtel Istanbul

DRINK
19. Taps

The Asian Shore (Üsküdar/Kadiköy)

When the ancient Greek Byzas asked an oracle where he should found his city, the oracle reputedly said 'opposite the blind', referring to the Chalcedonians who settled on the Asian side of the Bosphorus in the 7th century BC, ignoring the obvious advantages of the European shore. Perhaps they just wanted a quieter life. A 20-minute boat-trip from the teeming attractions of the European to the Asian shore indeed offers visitors a taste of Turkish life at a calmer pace, as well as the chance to boast that they have crossed between continents to find it.

It is only in the last two decades that the collection of villages on the Asian side of the Bosphorus have found themselves caught up in the mushroom-like growth of the city and recast as suburbs. The two main areas are Üsküdar to the north, which faces Beyoğlu across the water, and, south, Kadiköy, opposite the Old City. Primarily residential, the districts don't attract too many tourists. That doesn't stop locals flocking to the local bazaar in Kadiköy, by the Mustafa Iskele Mosque, or to what is one of the city's best street markets on nearby Kuşdili Sokak (Tuesday – food and clothes, Sunday – flea-market). Also close is Çiya,

a wonderfully unpretentious restaurant given the quality of its Anatolian cooking and in itself a destination worth the ferry trip.

Wandering up the shore to Üsküdar takes you past the Kız Kulesi – Maiden's Tower – an immensely popular landmark despite its lack or historical or architectural significance. Located just offshore on its own rocky outcrop and accessible by boat it is nonetheless a good place for a coffee and a pleasant spot from which to look at the Bosphorus. Round the bend is the beautiful Şemsi Paşa Mosque, one of the smallest, by star Ottoman architect Mimar Sinan.

You may
wish to
travel
further
afield as,
after the
intensity
of the
European
parts of Istanbul, a trip to the Asian shore often awakes impulses to escape and explore. One route northwards takes in the Asian Bosphorus villages, of which Kanlıca is one of the most charming, famous since the 17th century for its thick yoghurts and home to one the city's finest fish restaurants, Körfez.

In the other direction, the Kızıl Adalar – the Princes' Islands – lie off the south coast of Kadiköy. A collection of tranquil islands where superfluous Byzantine princes were once exiled (the more efficient Ottomans tended simply to strangle theirs), they have long attracted ethnically diverse settlers, bourgeois pleasure seekers from the city and assorted exiles, including, for a while, Leon Trotsky. But those with more extreme wanderlust need only venture into the idiosyncratically Teutonic form of Haydarpaşa station in Kadiköy, a gift from Kaiser Wilhelm, where they can catch trains for as far east as Tehran.

Ibuldere Baglarbasi Caddesi

Karibim Aziz Bey

nil Caddesi

ere Caddesi

Cavusdere Caddesi

Toptasi Caddesi

uyuk Selim Pasa Cad.

Hasan Bey

Eski Toptasi Caddesi

desi

Arakiyeci

Nuh Kuyusu Caddesi

si

si

0   250   500m

sleep...

The style revolution that has so recently shaped and inspired Istanbul's new generation of top restaurants and clubs is only just now beginning to penetrate into the rather staid hotel scene. A rash of boutique and style hotels currently on various drawing boards will pop up over the next few years. Nevertheless, even now there are at least a few excellent options despite the limited choice.

A major decision to make is choosing in which area to stay. Istanbul is a large city and can be time-consuming to traverse, so if your visit is short you should pick an appropriately located hotel. Those who wish primarily to immerse themselves in the historical sights will naturally want to stay in the Sultanahmet area. Here there is the usual flood of mediocre, chintzy hotels that exists in any touristy spot and only a few establishments stand out. The Four Seasons, perfectly located between the Hagia Sophia and the Sultanahmet Mosque, and elegantly housed in a former Ottoman prison, is, along with the Çirağan Palace, one of the city's two leading luxury hotels. Of course, the luxury comes at a price. The Empress Zoe and the Ibrahim Paşa Hotel, both nearby, are smaller, far more modest, but stylish and good value. Meanwhile the Eresin Crown, a smart four-star outfit, has the unique boast of being a museum hotel, exhibiting catalogued items from the Archaeology Museum's collection, including some fabulous busts and columns.

The hotels of the Pera district of Beyoğlu meanwhile offer a good compromise for those who wish to be in the midst of Istanbul's buzzing bar and restaurant district while remaining only a short taxi ride away from the sights of the old city. Here the excellent and newly opened Ansen Suite Hotel offers sleek sur-roundings and friendly service but only 10 suites. Just down the road Istanbul's most famous hotel, the Pera Palace, soldiers on, its Victorian glory increasingly ragged. Practically next door, Marmara Pera, belonging to Turkey's premier luxu-ry hotel group, has built a new, sleek, medium-sized offering replete with a rather stunning roof pool. Its larger, sister hotel, the Marmara Istanbul, is among the several five-star international hotels that cluster around the expansive wastes of Taksim Square in the north of Beyoğlu, catering principally for busi-ness trade.

The Çırağan Palace meanwhile sits on the shore of the Bosphorus, a little further up from the Dolmabahçe. A modern block with 310 rooms, built by owners Kempinski hotels, offers every extravagant luxury conceivable, but the real show-stopper is next door. The restored palace built by Sultan Abdülaziz in 1857 houses 12 spectacular suites, vast ballrooms and function rooms. Its central atrium boasts a wonderfully bizarre Egyptian-cum-late-Ottoman colour scheme and the world's heaviest chandelier (the largest is in the Dolmabahçe). The most expensive suite, which is of course accommodation fit for a sultan and overlooks the Bosphorus, is a snip at US$6,000 a night.

If however splendid isolation is more your thing, you may wish to head to the Asian shore, where the entrepreneurial Doors Group, owners of a slew of fashionable restaurants and nightclubs, have just converted a *yalı*, one of the late-Ottoman wooden mansions that line the Bosphorus, into A'jia, a coolly decorated, 16-room boutique hotel. Similarly the owners of the highly rated Kordon restaurant have converted an old *raki* distillery into the small, super-slick, design boutique hotel, Sumahan on the Water.

The rates range given is the price of a double room in low season to the price of a suite in the high season.

Our top ten hotels in Istanbul are:
1. Four Seasons
2. Çirağan Palace
3. Sumahan on the Water
4. A'jia Hotel
5. Ansen Suite Hotel
6. Ibrahim Paşa Hotel
7. Bentley Hotel
8. Bebek Hotel
9. Empress Zoe
10. Eresin Crown

Our top five hotels for style are:
1. Sumahan on the Water
2. A'jia Hotel
3. Ansen Suite Hotel
4. Bentley Hotel
5. Çirağan Palace

Our top five hotels for atmosphere are:
1. Sumahan on the Water
2. Ansen Suite Hotel
3. Çirağan Palace
4. Büyük Londra Hotel
5. Ibrahim Paşa Hotel

Our top five hotels for location are:
1. Four Seasons
2. Ayasofya Konakları
3. Yeşil Ev
4. Empress Zoe
5. Ibrahim Paşa Hotel

A'jia Hotel, Ahmet Rasim Paşa Yalısı,
Çubuklu Caddesi 27, Kanlıca
Tel: 0216 413 9300 www.ajiahotel.com
Rates: 430–1,100 YTL

Opened in summer 2005 A'jia is the latest and one of the most stylish additions to Istanbul's hotel scene. Run by the Doors Group, who operate a slew of fashionable restaurants and night-clubs (among them Vogue, Wan-na and Angelique), the 16-room establishment occupies a fabulous *yalı* (Ottoman wooden mansion) built by Ahmet Rasim Paşa on the Asian shore of the Bosphorus, near the village of Kanlıca, famous for its creamy yoghurts. Not that Ahmet Rasim Paşa would necessarily feel at home if he were to return. The interior has been given a sleek, contemporary and minimalist overhaul. White and beige predominate in the cool com-

munal areas, cream furniture and dark wood in the rooms. And one wonders what he would make of the mod cons – LCD TV screens, DVD players and WiFi – throughout the hotel. The hotel's location could be either a major attraction or seriously off-putting, depend-ing on your inclination. Although you can get to the Old City or Beyoğlu by water (nearby ferry or the hotel's own speedboat), or by taxi over the bridge, it's clearly not ideal for efficient sight see-ing. Conversely, the hotel is in a zone of calm, modern luxury away from the hectic city, with spectacular views of the Bosphorus.

Style 9, Atmosphere 8, Location 5

Ansen Suite Hotel, Meşrutiyet Caddesi 130, Tepebaşı
Tel: 0212 245 8808 www.ansensuite.com
Rates: 330–460 YTL

Another small, classy newcomer, the highly recommended 10-room Ansen Suite Hotel occupies an ornate, six-storey, late Ottoman building in the old hotel district of Pera (also called

Tepebaşı) in Beyoğlu. Successfully designed by architect Yylmaz Deðer to offer the comfortable feel of a private apartment, with the facilities of a hotel, the rooms are spacious, come with large TVs and dataports, and are contemporary without being pretentious. The addition of two little electric cooking rings in the kitchenette areas of the rooms is more symbolic than practical, given the many culinary attractions of Beyoğlu on its doorstep. The friendly staff and small but relaxed bar/lounge/dining/reception area contribute to a pleasantly informal atmosphere. There is also a small, eccentric private dining room with a glass front onto Meşrutiyet Caddesi, perfect for show-offs with a passion for dining, literally, in public. As there are only 10 rooms booking well in advance would be wise.

Style 9, Atmosphere 8, Location 8

Ayasofya Konakları, Soğukçeşme Sokak, Sultanhamet
Tel: 0212 513 3660 www.ayasofyapensions.com
Rates: 170–300 YTL

There are few hotels in the world that can boast of having three world-class cultural attractions on their doorstep. Most of those that can are in Sultanhamet and the Ayasofya Konakları (Ayasofya Mansions) is one of them. On an old cobbled lane next door to the Topkapı, right behind the Hagia Sophia and a small, weak child's stone throw from the Blue Mosque, its location is hard to better. Built in the 1980s by the Turkish Touring and Automobile Association, the Ayasofya Konakları (until recently the Ayasofya Pansiyonları – 'mansions' replacing 'pensions') was the first Ottoman boutique hotel. Unusually it is a row of pretty, pastel-coloured houses, with a total of 57 rooms and seven suites, built to exactly mimic the old Ottoman houses that once stood in their place. A separate building in pretty surroundings at the end of the street houses a restaurant and bar. The downsides are the tired, Ottoman-cum-19th-century-European chintzy décor (though renovations are underway) and the few mod cons.

Style 7, Atmosphere 6, Location 10

Bebek Hotel, Cevdet Paşa Caddesi 34, Bebek
Tel: 0212 358 2000 www.bebekhotel.com.tr
Rates: 280–300 YTL

Unsurprisingly few visitors end up staying as far from the old city or Beyoğlu as Bebek, the smartest of the village-cum-suburbs along the European shore of the Bosphorus. But if you prefer staying away from the bustle and picking your moments for going into town, then the Bebek Hotel might be for you. Set up by an ex-silk manufacturer in the 1950s, and completely refurbished in 2002, the 42-room Bebek Hotel is a peach, partly for the quality of its rooms, services, bar and restaurant, but mainly because of its terrific views of the Bosphorus, on whose shore it sits. Indeed, there's little point in staying here if you don't get a room

with a Bosphorus view. On a good day the hotel is 15 minutes by taxi from Beyoğlu, 30 minutes from Sultanahmet.

Style 8, Atmosphere 7, Location 5

Bentley Hotel, Halaskargazi Caddesi 75, Harbiye
Tel: 0212 291 7730 www.bentley-hotel.com
Rates: 280–560 YTL

The Bentley offers everything one would expect from Istanbul's first style hotel, modelled as it was by Milanese architects Piero Lissoni and Nicoletta Canesi, with stainless steel, dark wood and straight lines throughout, a smart fusion restaurant and nice, attached bar. All rooms have the full range of entertainment and communication mod cons but the suites are particularly cool and larger than most. Its location, however, sucks somewhat, being on a distinctly graceless busy main road, just north of Beyoğlu. Consequently it attracts business travellers as much as

tourists in search of style. But most places in Beyoğlu, Nişantaşı and the Bosphorus shore are only a fairly short taxi ride away.

Style 9, Atmosphere 7, Location 5

Büyük Londra Hotel, Meşrutiyet Caddesi 117, Tepebaşı
Tel: 0212 245 0670 www.londrahotel.net
Rates: 50–100 YTL

A serious option for those with a restricted budget and/or a developed sense of humour, the Londra is a charming and eccentric survivor of the high Victorian grandeur of Pera and a contemporary of its more famous near-neighbour, the Pera Palace. A showy, ornate façade, replete with a graceful row of caryatids, is

matched for attention by the recently renovated, period interior décor of the lobby and bar where the ceiling's elaborate plaster mouldings, enlivened by rather glaring colour choices, compete for attention with voluptuous chandeliers, loud wallpaper and, of course, caged parrots. The (few) staff, meanwhile, are more likely to be playing solitaire on computer than paying attention to anything in particular. Those are the highpoints. The rooms, though large, are worn (though a renovation programme is progressing), the bathrooms pretty basic (dodgy showers), and the breakfasts are eminently avoidable. The whole place is slightly reminiscent of those hotels in India that attempt to maintain the style and etiquette of the days of the Raj on shoestring budgets and only hazy, second-hand recollections of what they were in the first place.

Style 8, Atmosphere 8, Location 7

Çirağan Palace, Çirağan Caddesi 32, Beşiktaş
Tel: 0212 258 3377 www.ciraganpalace.com
Rates: 490–8,400 YTL

Sultan Abdülaziz built the Çirağan Palace in 1874 and killed himself inside it two years later, possibly because he'd made a mess of his reign, but more probably because he had psychic premonition of the bizarre colour scheme that the palace's current owners, the German Kempinski chain, would inflict on the palace's

magnificently OTT central, tiered atrium (home, incidentally, to the world's heaviest chandelier). Admittedly the place was a ruin before they did it up in 1986 and built a large, adjoining modern building to create a 310-room super-luxury hotel. The palace section, in fact, only houses 12 very expensive suites, but you are fortunate if you can afford them, as those that overlook the Bosphorus (especially the Sultan's Suite) are undoubtedly the most extraordinary sleeping quarters in the city. The rooms in the modern building aren't stellar, but the hotel's general all-round opulence, including an excellent small *hamam*, an amazing outdoor pool that appears to flow into the Bosphorus, superb restaurants and good bars, more than compensate. The location, dictated by Sultan Abdülaziz's wish for a little distance from his subjects, offers great Bosphorus views but isn't helpful for Old City sightseeing. Even if you don't end up staying here, the crazy palace section is worth a sightseeing visit anyway.

Style 9, Atmosphere 8, Location 7

Empress Zoe, Adliye Sokak 10, off Akbıyık Caddesi, Sultanahmet
Tel: 0212 518 2504 www.emzoe.com
Rates: 100–210 YTL

Small, stylish, perfectly placed and reasonably priced, the Empress Zoe is one of the best options in the Old City for those who

can't afford or don't want something as expensive or as formal as the Four Seasons. Named after a famous 11th-century Byzantine empress who got through a succession of lovers and husbands late in life, the hotel has 22 rooms, which are clean, prettily decorated and uncluttered – handy because they are quite small. Still you're better off spending time in the romantic, beautiful and leafy back garden, where you rest amid the ruins of a 15th-century *hamam*. Alternatively, you can dawdle on the rooftop terrace, which has superb views.

Style 8, Atmosphere 7, Location 9

Eresin Crown, Küçük Ayasofya Caddesi 40, Sultanahmet
Tel: 0212 638 4428 www.eresincrown.com.tr
Rates: 450–1,000 YTL

The Eresin Crown can, uniquely, style itself as a 'museum hotel', because dotted around the 59-roomed hotel are catalogued items from the Istanbul Archaeology Museum. Happily this is really just icing on a quality cake that makes the Eresin Crown the best luxury hotel in Sultanahmet behind its rather more luxurious and pricey near neighbour, the Four Seasons. The experience of the Eresin family, who run several hotels in the city, shows itself in the professional levels of service. All the smart, modern rooms have parquet flooring, Jacuzzis and several mod cons. The only letdown is the occasional lapse into kitsch, most

criminally in the ground floor 'Columns' bar, where several ancient columns are inveigled into a somewhat tasteless interior decoration scheme. Several bars and hotels in Sultanahmet have rooftop terraces with incredible views, including the Eresin Crown, but in fortuitous continuity with its antiquarian theme the hotel's rooftop terrace offers, in addition, a unique perspective on the substructure of the Hippodrome.

Style 7, Atmosphere 7, Location 8

Four Seasons, Tevkifhane Sokak 1, Cankurtaran
Tel: 0212 638 8200 www.fourseasons.com
Rates: 480–4,200 YTL

The most luxurious traditional hotel in Istanbul (unless you're forking out for the palace suites in the Çirağan), the Four Seasons was a popular hit (especially with wealthy Americans) from its

opening in 1994. Originally the building it occupies was an Ottoman prison built to service the nearby courts of law. Standards of service have considerably improved since those days, an irony that the original inmates would no doubt have enjoyed. The building's history has inadvertently bequeathed the hotel a kind of Ottoman minimalism with distinctive cultural features such as pointed arches and tall ceilings uncomplicated by the Turkish tendency towards the baroque (prisoners were not deemed worthy of baroque visual excitement). The 54 large rooms are beautiful and full of opulent furnishings, as well as TVs, CD players and so on. Service is excellent, helped by the hotel's intimate size. The location, between the Hagia Sophia and the Sultanahmet, is perfect. The food's not bad either – the Seasons Restaurant is one of the top places in town for sophisticated European cuisine. Inevitably top rates are charged for what is a top product.

Style 8, Atmosphere 8, Location 10

Ibrahim Paşa Hotel, Terzihane Sokak 5, Sultanahmet
Tel: 0212 518 0394 www.ibrahimpasha.com
Rates: 120–210 YTL

One of the best small hotels in Sultanahmet, and indeed Istanbul, the Ibrahim Paşa Hotel is an old, four-storey, late Ottoman house given a thorough, contemporary going over. Tastefully the management have neither ruined the period feel of the building by trying too hard, nor omitted to add modern features like WiFi through-

out the hotel, sleek LCD TVs in every one of its 19 well-decorated rooms and brightly coloured lampshades. Attractively tiled and patterned floors set the visual tone throughout, highlighted by the odd bit of statuary or large ornamental pot. Very reasonable prices, friendly and helpful staff, good Turkish-style breakfasts and proximity to the in-house pet (a large white Labrador) add to the general ambience, making the Ibrahim Paşa an excellent choice of hotel. Additionally it's round the corner from the Blue Mosque and so only minutes away from the Hagia Sophia and the Topkapı.

Style 8, Atmosphere 8, Location 8

Kybele Hotel, Yerebatan Caddesi 33–5, Sultanahmet
Tel: 0212 511 7766 www.kybelehotel.com
Rates: 120–170 YTL

A small hotel run by the friendly Akbaryrak family just up the road from the Hagia Sophia and the Blue Mosque distinguishes itself from myriad other small Istanbul hotels by being charmingly weird. Its bright turquoise, yellow and purple exterior colour scheme sets the tone. Inside and throughout the hotel hang

thousands of coloured-glass Turkish lamps, which can be found in any of the bazaars, the highpoint of a decidedly maximalist interior design, with armchairs, sofas and antiques of various periods all vying for attention. A small, very red, pink and ornate lounge area with original late 19th-century features is especially eye-catching. The Kybele's 16 rooms are fairly small and not especially modern (there is no internet or TV) but they have lovely en-suite bathrooms, and plenty of coloured illumination.

Style 7, Atmosphere 7, Location 8

Marmara Istanbul, Taksim Meydani, Taksim
Tel: 0212 251 4696   www.marmara.com.tr
Rates: 360–1,400 YTL

The Marmara Group is Turkey's leading hotel chain, with one luxury hotel in New York and a number in Istanbul within its portfolio. The five-star Marmara Istanbul is its largest but certainly

not its prettiest property, with around 400 rooms in a concrete tower overlooking the unlovely Taksim Square. If not picturesque, its location is at least central, so convenient for Beyoğlu and the Bosphorus, though not for the Old City. All the best places (and many that aren't so good) in Istanbul have great views, but the hotel's vertiginous height means that its outlook is especially impressive. Rooms are comfortable but suffer, like the whole establishment, from typical large-hotel-design tastelessness. However, that's balanced out by large-luxury-hotel benefits including the best gym in town, a nice outdoor pool and a good mini-*hamam*. Those who travel with bodyguards will want to book one of the penthouse presidential suites, which are frequented by Turkish presidents and prime ministers, where there are specially dedicated side rooms for travelling armed muscle.

Style 6, Atmosphere 7, Location 5

Marmara Pera, Meşrutiyet Caddesi 117, Tepebaşı
Tel: 0212 251 4646 www.themaramarahotel.com
Rates: 360–950 YTL

The Marmara Group's latest project, opened in late 2004, is its slickest yet, aimed squarely at the high-end tourist trade that the Marmara Istanbul lacks. Occupying a renovated 1970s building bang in the centre of Pera, its location is good for all-round visits. The post-minimalist interior design has something of the Ian Schrager about it, with the odd ornate touch, such as a crystal chandelier or brightly coloured leather chair, offsetting a predominantly dark colour scheme and spacious environment. Most rooms are decent in size and have good modern conveniences. The hotel's size – at 200 rooms – is just small enough to ensure

you don't get a sense of being anonymously swamped, which is common to large luxury hotels. Top marks, however, go to the astonishing rooftop pool reserved exclusively for hotel guests, which is almost good enough a reason in itself to book in.

Style 7, Atmosphere 6, Location 7

Pera Palace, Meşrutiyet Caddesi 98, Tepebaşı, Beyoğlu
Tel: 0212 251 4560 www.perapalas.com
Rates: 300–560 YTL

To stay in the Pera Palace is to value historical significance over physical luxury and only for the ascetic. You never know, that might be your bag. The hotel has history and anecdotal interest in spades. People nowadays pretend not to be excited by such things but generally they're lying. Built by the owners of the Orient

Express and designed by French architect Alexander Vallaury, the hotel has, since 1891, allowed a host of the rich, famous and regal to shack up under its roof, including King Edward VIII, various Shahs and, of course, King Zog of Albania. The hotel management also includes the 'famous spy Cicero' in its list of notable guests, overlooking the fact that no spy worth his salt would be caught dead being famous (or in fact would be caught and killed if they were famous). Kemal Atatürk had a suite here, which is preserved as he left it, save for the unhappy addition of lots of tacky portraits of the great man. Meanwhile Agatha Christie wrote part of *Murder in the Orient Express* here. As with the Büyük Londra, the communal areas have mostly retained their elegance or interest while the rooms have rather gone to seed. The ancient lift (the first electric lift in the city) is still smartly polished and functioning. Also interesting are the dining room and central atrium, with its slightly sinister mezzanine, whose small, moveable, internal windows allow discreet spying on people below. The rooms, though large, are very tired and the bathrooms are in urgent need of modernization. But if it was good enough for King Zog…

Style 6, Atmosphere 7, Location 7

Richmond Hotel, İstiklal Caddesi 445, Beyoğlu
Tel: 0212 252 5460   www.richmondhotels.com.tr
Rates: 280–420 YTL

With decent-sized, clean and well-designed contemporary rooms, an expansive lobby, a bar and rooftop restaurant with outstanding views of the old city and the Bosphorus, and profes-

sional levels of service, the Richmond is a high-quality, if slightly characterless accommodation option. Crucially, however, it's the only hotel on the entire length of İstiklal Caddesi, the pedestrianized artery of Beyoğlu. Located towards İstiklal's southern end, the Richmond is only a short walk away from many of Beyoğlu's hotspots, including Sofayali Sokak, which is just over the road, and is also close to Galata, from where you pick up a cab for the short ride to the Old City. So as with the hotels in Pera it is ideally located for those planning to split their time between sightseeing and experiencing more modern pleasures.

Style 6, Atmosphere 6, Location 8

Sumahan on the Water, Kuleli Caddesi 51, Çengelköy
Tel: 0216 422 8000   www.sumahan.com
Rates: 260–530 YTL

Opened in May 2005, Sumahan on the Water is, like A'jia, a fantastically stylish renovation of an old building on the Asian shore of the Bosphorus. The Sumahan was a 19th-century Ottoman distillery that made *rakı*, bought by the present owner's grandfather. Consequently the hotel has the kind of spaciousness and

cool aesthetic common to converted industrial buildings in London and New York but rare in Istanbul. The conversion is superb and the rooms are outstanding throughout. All 20 of them have lovely Bosphorus views, and are achingly cool in design with modern fireplaces, fashionable furniture and all entertainment and communication mod cons. There are 13 very spacious suites; a number of them are duplexes and even have their own small terrace gardens where you can sit on the lawn and enjoy the vista. Downstairs is Kordon, an excellent fish restaurant, belonging to the same owner. As with A'jia the location could be either a dream or a hassle. The hotel's private launch will ferry you across the Bosphorus to Kabatas on the European side in 15 minutes, from where you can easily pick up a cab into town. So that's probably more dream than hassle then.

Style 9, Atmosphere 7, Location 7

**Swissôtel Istanbul – The Bosphorus,
Bayıldım Caddesi 2 Maçka**
Tel: 0212 326 1100 http://istanbul.swissotel.com
Rates: 250–1,330 YTL

Until the very recent arrival of Istanbul's first design hotels, travellers have had to choose between chintzy hotels in Sultanahmet, dives in Beyoğlu or the big luxury chain hotel clustered together in Maçka Park, the old gardens of the Dolmabahçe Palace, just north of Taksim Square. Of the latter the 600-room Swissôtel is the best, located on a wooded hilltop with truly magnificent views of the city and the Bosphorus, oozing with five-star luxury. Several marble quarries have been emptied to fit out the hotel while amenities include 16 different restaurants, Turkish baths, spas, saunas, fitness centres, an indoor pool, tennis courts, a jogging path (extremely rare in the city), etc, etc. The rooms themselves are decently sized. But you will pay for enjoying this enviable list of comforts by having to endure the standard, large hotel chintzy naffness and anonymous atmosphere.

Style 7, Atmosphere 6, Location 6

Taxim Suites, Cumhuriyet Caddesi 49, Taksim
Tel: 0212 254 7777 www.taximsuites.com
Rates: 250–350 YTL

Though aimed primarily at the long-stay, business traveller, for whom its location on the fringes of the commercial district is convenient, the Taxim Suites does attract some tourists. It's a stylish and very professional apartment hotel, which, from a

tourist's point of view, has just been trumped by Ansen Suite Hotel, which offers a better location and a cooler, less formal service style. However, the apartments at Taksim are smoothly designed and well equipped so that if you decide you like the city so much that you're going to extend that long weekend into a long-stay, this is the place to be. The Miyako Suite's minimal Japanese style, and the fifth-floor penthouses, the Bosphorus and Taxsim Suites, are very spacious and swanky.

Style 6, Atmosphere 5, Location 5

Yeşil Ev, Kabasakal Caddesi 5, Sultanahmet
Tel: 0212 517 6785 www.ayasofyapensions.com
Rates: 200–350 YTL

Another Ottoman boutique hotel, owned like the Ayasofya Konakları by the Turkish Touring Association, the Yeşil Ev is a large, restored Ottoman wooden mansion (its name means Green House). Like its sister establishment it is amazingly located near the Hagia Sophia and the Blue Mosque, but also suffers from being a little kitsch and tired in places. However, it's very popular with its loyal clientele and the 19 rooms are often booked up well in advance. The best room in the place, the Pasha's Room, is worth paying out the extra for, with its opulent fabrics and décor, and an en-suite mini-Turkish bath. As well as the look of the exterior, the highlight of the Yeşil Ev is the lovely and relatively spacious garden at the back, where meals are served and drinks can be enjoyed calmly while contemplating the spectacular surrounding domes and minarets that flank the hotel.

Style 6, Atmosphere 7, Location 10

eat...

If you hate history, monuments and sightseeing, have a deep-seated aversion to nightclubs and bars, aren't remotely interested in shopping and are allergic to all physical activities you could still have a good time in Istanbul by eating. In doing so you would be following in a great imperial tradition, for in the pursuit of gastronomic indulgence the Ottoman sultans led from the front, their vast kitchens, at their height, employing 1,300 staff to blend traditions, ingredients and flavours culled from all corners of the empire.

Sadly Ottoman chefs, strict adherents to the thesis that knowledge is power, never wrote anything down and the few restaurants that claim to purvey *saray* (palace) cuisine with its unusual combinations of sweet and savoury tastes, including Asitane and the elegant Feriye, make great bones of their historical detective work in piecing together recipes.

The basic, though delicious, Turkish diet has rather humbler origins. Its meat-centricity stretches back to the nomadic past when Turkic tribes took their larders with them in the form of assorted hoofed animals. The grilled meat tradition is upheld in countless *kebabçi* (kebab joints) and *ocakabaşı* (where the food will be grilled in front of you), most of which are excellent. Nor is the millennia old culinary tradition static – the doner kebab was only invented in 1867, in Western Turkey. Nonetheless, a few famous and more pricey establishments vie for the reputation of making the best kebab in Istanbul (and by extension the world), prime among them: Beyti, Develi, Hacı Abdullah and Hamdi.

Then there are the *meyhanes*, exponents of the Mediterranean tradition of the *meze*. Here the tiny area of Azmalımescit, near the bottom of İstiklal Caddesi,

offers some of the best including Refik and Yakup 2, where bottles of *rakı* and a hubbub accompany myriad dishes of fish, meat and vegetable preparations. More raucous, slightly less genteel but immensely popular are the many *meyhanes* that pack

nearby Nevizade Sokak. Quite different, but equally authentic, is Çiya, an unpretentious but superb restaurant on the Asian side that produces masterpieces of Anatolian cooking.

The key to the quality of these traditional Turkish establishments is the freshness of the ingredients, a quality unsurprisingly also prevalent in Istanbul's many fish restaurants, of which Balıkçı Sabahattin, Doğa Balık, Körfez and Poseidon are the best. For the ultimate in freshness and personal choice, however, head to the fish market by Galata Bridge, pick your (possibly still wriggling) piscine date for the night and walk round the corner where a nice man in a hat will grill it for you.

Finally there is the raft of über-stylish new restaurants that have opened over the last five years, offering international and fusion cuisine, which are magnets for Istanbul's brightly dressed-up young things (and their older, wealthier, sugar daddies). Changa, one of the first and still one of the best, is joined by Vogue, with its spectacular views, Wan-na, with its spectacular lighting displays, Lokanta, Loft, Ulus 29 and new entrant 360°. The standard of food is high in all these restaurants, and is generally more than matched by the visual delight on offer.

The price given is for three courses and half a bottle of wine per person.

Our top ten restaurants in Istanbul are:
1. Çiya
2. Balıkcı Sabahattin
3. Lokanta
4. Changa
5. Feriye
6. Borsa
7. Refik
8. Beyti
9. Korfez
10. Galata House

Our top five restaurants for food are:
1. Çiya
2. Lokanta
3. Balıkcı Sabahattin
4. Feriye
5. Changa

Our top five restaurants for service are:
1. Borsa
2. Poseidon
3. Feriye
4. Seasons Restaurant
5. Lokanta

Our top five restaurants for atmosphere are:
1. Nevizade Sokak
2. Refik
3. Galata House
4. Lokanta
5. Sunset Grill & Bar

360°, 7th and 8th Floor, İstiklal Caddesi Mısır Apartmanı, Beyoğlu
Tel: 0212 251 1042 www.360istanbul.com
Open: 7pm–midnight daily   85 YTL

Set up by people who clearly felt that Istanbul didn't quite
have enough places with fantastic views, 360° occupies a
purpose-built floor above a lovely, ornate period building

slap-bang in the middle of İstiklal Caddesi. Club/bar/restau-
rant 360°, like the similar all-in-one attractions of
Lokanta/Nu Pera/Nu Terras in nearby Pera, is helping
Beyoğlu rival the Bosphorus as a top nightlife spot, even for
the super-smart, trendy and glamorous, and with more taste
and less vulgarity. The kitchen-supremo at 360° is Mike
Norman, ex-head chef of the Çırağan Palace, who's put
together a menu with a fusion of global styles, all wonderfully tasty and expertly prepared. Some of the dishes take
account of the club/bar environment and, like whatever
chewing gum that was, are great for sharing. Others you
can keep all to yourself. The attractions aren't confined to
the plate before you – there are plenty of well-grilled, or
tanned at least, shapely specimens (male and female) among
the clientele.

Food 8, Service 8, Atmosphere 8

Next to the beautiful Church of Christ in Chora in the
west of the Old City, Asitane is in the basement of the
Kariye Hotel. In a smartish, formal setting the restaurant
serves up what it describes as classic Ottoman *saray*
(palace) cuisine. But Ottoman cooks never wrote anything
down. There is a famous anecdote told of the pastry chef of
a visiting French royal who met his Turkish counterpart in
the imperial kitchens and hoped to pick up a recipe or two.
As they began talking the Frenchman pulled out his measur-
ing spoons, weight and scales and notebook, aiming for a

certain precision of information exchange, whereupon the
Turk seized them and threw them out of the nearest win-
dow in disgust, pointing out that cooking is an art depend-
ent on the constant application of finely tuned sensitivities
and judgements, not a question of robotically following a
set of instructions. Consequently the chefs at Asitane and
Feriye, the two Ottoman restaurants in this selection,
spend as much time scouring historical accounts of imperial
feasts as sourcing ingredients. Much of the current menu,
for example, is a recreation of dishes served up at the
circumcision feast of Süleyman the Magnificent's sons,
including almond soup and meats stewed with fruits and

seasoned with cinnamon and honey. Purists find this is all a bit faux-Ottoman and there is certainly theatricality at play. Nevertheless, the tastes are worth trying.

Food 7, Service 7, Atmosphere 7

Balıkcı Sabahattin, Seyti Hasan Kuyu Sokak 50, off Cankurtaran
Tel: 0212 458 1824
Open: midday–1am daily   65 YTL

The best fish restaurant in the Old City is also one of the best in Greater Istanbul, drawing in customers from all over to sit, in summer, in its pretty, shaded outdoor, cobbled space that is framed by the decaying old wooden houses of Sultanahmet. To make things simple there's no menu; instead, a profusion of *meze* dishes are brought to you by

the smartly attired waiters, after which a selection of fresh fish on ice is paraded before you so you can pick your piscine date for the evening. Not any old selection, either. Before they've got anywhere near your table they've been vetted by Balıkcı Sabahattin's proprietor, Mr Sabahattin Cankurtaran, who is up at the crack of dawn trawling the fish markets to get his hands on the day's best catches. Excellent food in a charming setting – therefore reservations are essential.

Beyti, Orman Sokak 8, Florya
Tel: 0212 663 2990
Open: 11.30am–11.30pm. Closed Mondays.   75 YTL

Beyti Güler is a legend in his own lunchtime, probably the only living Turk to have a kebab named after him (the Beyti kebab obviously – minced lamb with garlic and peppers served in filo pastry). His family opened their first restau-

rant in 1945, quickly gaining a reputation for serving a nicely done bit of meat. Beyti opened his current establishment in the 1970s and it is, in kebab terms, the Holy of Holies, a 3,000-square-metre palace of carnivorous pleasure with 11 dining rooms and five kitchens. Other places grow their own vegetables, Beyti rears its own lamb. Beyti himself oversees the selection and preparation of the meat, but if you're lucky he might totter over and say hello, as he has done with a succession of the world's great and good that have dropped by while in the city. Damn right too, because after the substantial taxi-ride to reach the place (it's out near the airport somewhere) it's only polite that he makes some kind of reciprocal gesture. Anyway it's not Beyti's conversational abilities that have charmed the world but his lovely tender chops, which you should make a point of trying. Beyti also does a nice line in faded politicians. Two of his most famous customers have been Richard Nixon and Jimmy Carter. Essential stop for enthusiastic meat eaters (unless you're an aspiring US president).

Food 8/9, Service 8, Atmosphere 8

Borsa, Istanbul Convention and Exhibition Centre (Lütfi Kırdar Kongere Merkezi), Darülbedai Caddesi 6, Harbiye
Tel: 0212 232 4201
Open: midday–3.30pm, 6.30pm–midnight daily   85 YTL

Widely considered to be one of the best Turkish restaurants in town, this Borsa is a chic part of an old, family-run chain, begun 75 years ago. The location is a bit of a duffer, being the unappealing Istanbul Convention and Exhibition Centre in Harbiye, just north of Taksim Square. Nevertheless Istanbul's well-heeled professionals flock in from the surrounding smart neighbourhoods and regularly fill out the restaurant's 500-person capacity, giving the place

a convivial buzz. The service is super slick and highly attentive for such a large place and the food, too, is top quality, with the usual Turkish menu of *meze* followed by typical meat and fish dishes. The classic Turkish aubergine dish, *Imam bayıldı*, meaning 'the Imam fainted' (because it was so

57

good rather than because of food poisoning), the oven-cooked lamb (*kuzu tandır*) and the steamed sea-bass (*levrek buğulamanın*) are perennial favourites. Reservations are essential.

Food 8, Service 9, Atmosphere 8

Changa, Sıraselviler Caddesi 87/1, Taksim
Tel: 0212 249 1348
Open: 6pm–1am (2am Fri/Sat) daily
Closed Sundays.   80 YTL

One of the pioneers and still one of the leaders of Istanbul's super-fashionable fusion cuisine revolution, Changa is a destination for Istanbul's smart set. Through an imposing entrance to a beautifully detailed Art Nouveau building in the large, busy and unlovely Sıraselviler Caddesi, you find the attractive and slickly contemporary restaurant

occupying several floors. Diners on the ground level will not only enjoy the long, stylish bar, but also watching the kitchen staff at work in the basement below, thanks to the large Perspex porthole thoughtfully set in the floor by the designer. It provides a visceral reminder of the harsh reality of socio-economic relations, perhaps, but is eye-catching nonetheless. The food, the aforementioned staff are busy preparing as you watch them, is excellent. A menu designed

by well-known chef Peter Gordon, formerly of the Sugar
Club, now of the Providores in London, lives up to its
fusion label mixing south-east Asian and European tastes
and ingredients, as in, for example, the delicious 'wasabi and
salmon tortellini with grilled porcini and creamed lemon-
grass sauce'. The prices aren't bad, either. Changa offers an
excellent entrée to the flavours of New Istanbul.

Food 9, Service 8, Atmosphere 8

**Cibalikapı, Abdülezel Paşa Caddesi 7, Cibali –
Haliç (winter)**
Tarihi Moda İskelesi Yolu Moda, Kadıköy (summer)
Tel: 0212 533 2846 (winter), 0216 348 9363 (summer)
Open: 5pm–midnight (2am Fri/Sat) daily   60 YTL

In the winter months Cibalikapı occupies a sweet, ram-
shackle olden wooden building on the Golden Horn. A
maritime décor of glass buoys, fishing nets and lobster pots
crowd the warm and intimate wooden interior. Traditional
old Turkish and Greek tunes play in the background, adding
to the slightly nostalgic atmosphere(without being naff)
while you pick your dishes, all made, as with all the top fish
restaurants in the city, with the freshest fish bought that
day at the fish markets. Sıdıka Karaman, the owner of
Cibalikapı, meanwhile has just opened up a summer venue,

to cater to discerning Istanbullis' taste for seasonal dining. If it's summer many make a point of not eating indoors. Located in the pleasant Asian suburb of Moda, the summer venue is charming despite the lack of a sea view. In both you get all the classics, best accompanied by a few glasses of *rakı*.

Food 8, Service 8, Atmosphere 8

Çiya, Güneşlibahçe Sokak 43–44, Kadiköy

Tel: 0216 418 5115 www.ciya.com.tr
Open: 11am–10pm daily   40 YTL

A restaurant worth crossing the continents for. This won't immediately be apparent as Çiya, only a few streets away from the ferry port in Kadiköy, is unassuming in appearance and most of clientele look as if they've only crossed the road to get there. Which they have. Popular with local workers who come here for lunch, Çiya serves up Anatolian cooking with nuance and sophistication. There are in fact two Çiyas – Çiya Kebapçı, a meat joint with a

dizzying array of kebabs, and Çiya Sofrası, the one I'm talking about, which serves the rarer rural specialities. Anatolia's assimilation of culinary traditions from neighbouring countries is evident in Çiya's selection of unusual tasting stews, meat and vegetable dishes that tend to be accompanied by light sauces which have powerful, herby tastes. Desserts are equally unusual, including creamy puddings with the odd surprising savoury ingredients, and candied fruit. The Anatolian chief chef comes from Gaziantep and includes many specialities from that area in his cooking. Rather than try to navigate the bewildering and alien choices try asking the helpful staff to bring a tasting selection.

Food 9/10, Service 8, Atmosphere 7/8

Develi, Samatya Balık Pazarı, Gümüşyüzük Sokak 7, Mustafa Paşa
Tel: 0212 529 0833
Open: midday–midnight daily   60 YTL

Since 1912 the smart Develi has been delivering spicy kebabs and other traditionally southeast Anatolian dishes to the city. Its excellent reputation has survived the decades intact and the restaurant occupies a large, ornamental wooden building on the long costal road that stretches along the Sea of Marmara from the Old City towards the airport. The drive is worth it, an opinion shared by the clientele who come from miles around. Perennial favourites are the *çiğ köfte* (like steak tartar) and the delicious *keme* kebab (cooked with apple and walnuts). The expansive

restaurant includes in its portfolio of dining locations a large terrace overlooking the Sea of Marmara, which is where the action is in the summer, especially if you're a ship-spotter with a particular fascination with tankers and cargo vessels, which tend to be liberally strewn across the vista.

Food 8, Service 8, Atmosphere 7

Doğa Balık, Akarsu Yokuşu Caddesi 46, Cihangir
Tel: 0212 293 9143 www.doga-balik.com
Open: midday–2am daily   65 YTL

Another of Istanbul's top fish restaurants, Doğa Balık is found above the Hotel Villa Zurich in trendy central Cihangir, which locals describe as an odd location for a fish restaurant as it's 'in town' as opposed to being on the seashore, which is all of five minutes away. Happily this means it's in easy reach if you're hanging around Beyoğlu. A superb view across the water to Sultanahmet is merely a bonus. The real draw is the simply served but delicious *meze* and fish. A particular speciality is vegetarian *meze*, including an impressive variety of wilted herbs in olive oil and other dressings (which makes Doğa Balık an excellent vegetarian option, too). As for the fish, try some cooked simply with onions and herbs…

Feriye, Feriye Sarayı, Çirağan Caddesi 124, Oratköy
Tel: 0212 227 2216
Open: midday–3pm, 7pm–midnight daily   90 YTL

The closest you can get, in restaurant terms, to the world
of the late Ottoman elites is Feriye, set in a beautifully
restored and particularly grand old police station within
palatial grounds that once belonged to the Çirağan. Set up
by celebrity chef Vedat Başaran, Feriye, like Asitane (see
above), serves up *saray* (palace) cuisine, playing detective to
unearth old Ottoman and even Byzantine techniques, often
applied with a contemporary twist, but with rather greater
swishness and formality. A seasonal menu is dominated by
whatever fresh ingredients are available. Signature dishes

include air-dried beef wrapped in vine leaves and homemade *mantı* (ravioli) filled with pine nuts and fish served
with a pepper '*tarator*'. For the best in succulent meat try
the grilled, milk-fed lamb served on charcoal grilled
aubergine puree with yoghurt and *perve pilav* with raisins.
This is also an excellent place to try a typically Turkish
dessert, *tavuk göğsü* (chicken breast pudding), which is considerably nicer than it sounds. Feriye provides excellent,
distinctively Turkish cuisine served in a turn-of-the-last-

century, high European, opulent setting.

Food 8/9, Service 9, Atmosphere 8

Flamm, Sofayali Sokak 16, Asmalımescit
Tel: 0212 245 7604   www.flamm-ist.com
Open: 11am–2am daily   80 YTL

A lovely restored 19th-century, high-ceilinged building provides the setting for the modern and elegant Flamm, the
latest arrival on Sofayali Sokak, a foodie's paradise on a
small Istanbul side street. Set up by hotelier Irfan Kuris,
Flamm offers a more formal option than the *meyhanes* next
door, as well as alternative tastes, serving up a mixture of
classic European and Turkish dishes, with prosciutto, steak
and kebabs all floating around (although happily not in the
same dish). Though all the courses are excellent, the puddings are fantastic and the warm chocolate cake, baked on
the premises, might well be the best in the city.

Food 7, Service 7, Atmosphere 7

**Galata Bridge Fish Grills, Galata Bridge,
Kulesi Sokak 61, Galata**
Tel: 0212 245 1861
Open: midday–midnight. Closed Mondays.   35 YTL

Kumkapı (see below) used to be the best place to go if you wanted nice fresh fish, simply prepared. Now for that experience you might try heading for the fish market on the Beyoğlu side of Galata Bridge, buying a fish of your choice and walking round the corner where, in a few crotchety buildings on the edge of a rare patch of grass, sprinkled with a few trees, you can find a few men with grills who will cook up your catch for you. Of course they have stock of their own, so you don't actually have to buy the fish yourself and run the embarrassing risk of turning up with a dud that their expert eye would have spotted a nautical mile off. It's especially nice at night, when you can sit at candlelit tables among the trees.

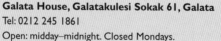

Food 7, Service 7, Atmosphere 9

Galata House, Galatakulesi Sokak 61, Galata
Tel: 0212 245 1861
Open: midday–midnight. Closed Mondays.   50 YTL

When it comes to charming eccentricity Galata House beats every other Istanbul restaurant hands down. Run by the multi-skilled Nadire and Mete Göktuğ, architects with a strong sideline in cooking, it occupies an attractively worn 18th-century building just off Galata Tower that used to the old British prison. There, under a special dispensation from the sultans, the British incarcerated their own errant subjects. In what is the certainly the most distinctive interior design scheme among the city's many restaurants, the Göktuğs have wisely preserved those poor souls' doodled graffiti along with passages of peeling paint from the period. Particularly notable are the naïve but powerful renderings of various wardens along with a selection of their attractively shaped hats. The simple, homely furniture and decoration combined with the Göktuğ's friendliness soon dispense any thoughts of imprisonment. Though popular at times, if you come on a weekday evening, especially in winter, the place may well be empty. No matter, Mete will sit down and

have a chat while Nadire will rustle up the menu's Georgian, Russian and Tartar delicacies, all from her Crimean homeland. Then, if you're really lucky, she'll have a tinkle on the ivories, throwing wild Georgian songs into the mix.

Food 8, Service 8, Atmosphere 9

**Hacı Abdullah, Sakızağacı Caddesi 17,
off İstiklal Caddesi, Beyoğlu**
Tel: 0212 293 8561
Open: 11am–10.30pm daily   50 YTL

Having been open for nearly 120 years Hacı Abdullah is the city's oldest restaurant, serving up Turkish and Ottoman delicacies while the Ottomans were still in rude health, busy being paranoid and murdering each other. Hacı Abdullah doesn't wear its age on its sleeve, however. Its large, spacious interior has a contemporary but warm feel, thanks to the wall-to-ceiling wood and the rows upon rows of huge jars of brightly coloured, pickled vegetables. If you go, sit in the back room, which is the nicest. The food – *meze*, soups, stews, kebabs and roasted meats – and service is universally good. The place is easily accessible, so if you're in town just for a few days and looking for an easy to find, quality Turkish restaurant, Hacı Abdullah is a good choice. No alcohol is served and the place closes earlier than many of its rivals, so lunch could be the best option here.

Food 8, Service 8, Atmosphere 7

Hamdi, Kalcin Sokak 17, Tahmis Caddesi, Eminönü
Tel: 0212 512 5424
Open: 11.30am–midnight daily   45 YTL

Just on the south side of Galata Bridge and round the corner from the Egyptian Bazaar is Hamdi, one of Istanbul's premier purveyors of deluxe kebabs, on a par with the legendary Beyti. The principal reason for the quality is the consistent and expert attention of Mr Hamdi, who, along with his bristly moustache, keeps a dictatorial eye on all proceedings. The dishes from south east Anatolia (the original home of the kebab) include among them the lovely *fıstık* kebab, made with pistachio nuts, *erikli* kebab, with plums, and the *testi* kebab, made with lamb's testicles and very nice they are too. In summer you'll sit up on the rooftop terrace with its nice views across the Golden Horn toward the Galata Tower. The delicious food engenders a passionate and loyal following among local professionals and discerning carnivores across the city.

Food 8/9, Service 7, Atmosphere 7

Körfez, Körfez Caddesi 78, Kanlıca
Tel: 0216 413 4314
Open: midday–4pm, 7pm–midnight daily   90 YTL

This is one of the city's favourite fish restaurants and you can see why. Körfez (gulf) is in the beautiful Asian Bosphorus village of Kanlica, just opposite the imposing castle of Rumeli Hisar. There, outside the fabulous and surreal Edwards of Hisar, a gentleman's tailors that appears to have walked out of a page of Jeeves and Wooster, Körfez's motorboat will pick you up and ferry you across the Bosphorus. Once at the restaurant you can enjoy the view from the splendid riverside garden. The fish is seasonal and excellent – sea bass baked in salt is the famous house dish.

It's a simple formula but it works, drawing people to the restaurant from across the city. Körfez is a good choice if you fancy a small adventure and want to impress someone, or indeed yourself. Reservations are essential.

Kumkapı Meyhanes, Kumkapı
Tel: none
Open: most are open midday–2am daily   45 YTL

An old Greek and Armenian fishing district on the Sea of Marmara, Kumkapı, a brief taxi ride from the centre of the Old City, was for a while one of the best places to go in town for fish fans. Simplicity was a virtue, with the clutch of *meyhanes* that opened up around a lovely square serving fresh fish in a simple and lively environment. When it's warm, and all the seating is outside, the place still has a good buzz, but popularity with tourists has brought a certain naffness, and a reputation for its restaurateurs being a little dishonest, short-changing customers, bringing you dishes you didn't order, and so on. However, some among the many establishments are fine, and if you're in the area and hungry it's still worth a try. Those like Patara, off the main square, are recommended. The food is a straightforward fish *meze* and can be good.

Food 6/7, Service 5, Atmosphere 7

● **Loft, Istanbul Convention & Exhibition Centre
(Lütfi Kırdar Kongere Merkezi), Darülbedai Caddesi 6,
Harbiye**
Tel: 0212 219 6384
Open: midday (5pm Sat)–2am. Closed Sundays.   80 YTL

Run by the New York trained chef Umut Özkanca, whose
father owns Borsa one level up in the Istanbul Convention
and Exhibition Centre, Loft is frequented by celebs, business-
men, the generally stylish and other trend-setters among the
city's haute bourgeoisie. The atmosphere is contemporary

chic, set up by a beautiful winter garden at the entrance and sustained inside by a cool décor replete with geometric furniture arrangements, sculptural lights, leather banquettes and resident DJs. Accordingly the menu is cool fusion, expertly done and served up by attentive staff. Slick, modern and good.

Food 8/9, Service 8, Atmosphere 8

Lokal, Müeyyet Sokak 9, Tünel
Tel: 0212 245 5743 www.lokal-istanbul.com
Open: midday–midnight (1am Fri/Sat) daily   40 YTL

Trend-central, as you can tell from the toy Transformers (robots in disguise) on every table and the knowingly kitsch, retro decoration, Lokal is small but immensely popular with the city's young and cool. Being handily located just off Istiklal and Sofayali Sokak helps. The food is global, prepared in an open kitchen, varying from good, fresh, homemade burgers to Pad Thai via every other culinary continent going. There is often a good atmosphere here as Lokal is something of a meeting point for a crowd who tend to know each other – it can get quite boisterous, especially as the cocktails are good. Ask for the table with Optimus Prime, the best conversationalist among the toy robots.

Food 7/8, Service 7, Atmosphere 8

Tied with Changa for the title of best fusion restaurant in town, Lokanta is a super-stylish establishment on the ground floor at the core of the Nu Pera building, which houses Nu Club in the basement for clubbing outside the summer season, and Nu Terras above for dining during the summer months. Here even the head chef, Mehmet Gürs, is a fusion, a Turko-Finn, so the catholic approach to global cuisines is more natural than contrived, with a large range of dishes from pizza and pasta to meat and fish main courses served with innovative sauces varying from spicy, Asian concoctions to more creamy European ones. The decoration meanwhile mixes up exposed period brickwork with a few contemporary industrial touches. The affluent, smart set, starting from the late-20s upwards in age, flock to the place, so book if you want a place at the table.

Food 9, Service 8, Atmosphere 8

Open only during the summer months, the smart Mia Mensa has

a lovely location, sharing a waterside terrace with Aşşk Café on the nightlife strip of Kuruçeşme. The cuisine is Italian, excellently prepared with the freshest ingredients accompanied by a decent wine list and good service. Though nice for lunch when the profusion of blue parasols offer shade while the Bosphorus basks in the sunshine, the place is enchanting at night, especially on a clear night, when you can watch the tankers sailing by as you enjoy your antipasti.

Food 8, Service 8, Atmosphere 8

Nevizade Sokak, off Çicek Pasajı, off İstiklal Caddesi, Beyoğlu
Tel: 0212 243 1219   60 YTL
Open: most restaurants are open midday–midnight/2am daily

Not a single restaurant but a narrow street that runs off the covered fish market, just off Çicek Pasajı, a lovely 19th-century passage full of attractive-looking restaurants but, unfortunately, also touts trying to lure passing tourists in. The 20 or so more down-to-earth but toutless *meyhanes* on Nevizade Sokak pull in tourists, too, but the generous helping of locals who fill the tables that line both sides of the street dilutes them. When the place gets going there's a great energy, full of noise and action from waiters scurrying back and forth with huge trays of *meze* while *fasıl* musicians ply their trade. The *meyhanes* are invariably good, with slight variations between them being a bias towards dishes from one region or another, or a particular reputation for good live music. Take your time strolling by and pick one that takes your fancy. A good place to head to on your first night in the city, just to make sure you get into the swing of things quickly.

Food 7/8, Service 7, Atmosphere 9

Niş, Abdi İpekçi Caddesi 44/3, Nişantaşı
Tel: 0212 258 3627
Open: midday–midnight daily   70 YTL

At the heart of the chicville that is Nişantaşı is Niş, a restaurant/bar where locals often seek sustenance to fuel another few hours of vital shopping. The atmosphere's

buzzy and energetic, and the clientele suitably elegant. The menu never stands still, changing almost daily, but is always rich and varied, with a mixture of Turkish and European tastes, dishes and options for those calorie-controlled fashionistas searching for a special salad as well as hungry visitors looking for something more substantial. Live jazz and cocktails draw people to the upstairs bar, as does the happy hour on Saturdays.

Food 7/8, Service7, Atmosphere 7

Pandeli, Mısır Çarşısı 1, Eminönü
Tel: 0212 527 3909
Open: midday–4pm. Closed Sundays.   80 YTL

An Istanbul classic, Pandeli occupies a series of rooms above the riotous bustle and assault on the senses that is the Egyptian Bazaar. From the ancient doorway through which you have to pass, to the terrific, decorative, blue and white tiles, Pandeli has one of the most atmospheric and quintessentially Old Stamboul settings one can imagine. As a result of this and its location, Pandeli attracts droves of tourists and the management and staff take full advantage. Reports suggest that the staff can be incredibly pushy for tips while also being rude, though I didn't find that myself. The food also receives mixed reviews, but it is straight Turkish food normally done competently but not outstandingly. But the location and the feeling of the place are superb, so other

deficiencies may be worth putting up with, and if the staff get uppity then just be ruder and bossier than they are. Note that Pandeli serves lunch only.

Food 7, Service 4, Atmosphere 9

Poseidon, Küçük Bebek, Cevdat Paşa Caddesi 58, Bebek
Tel: 0212 263 2997
Open: midday–2am daily   85 YTL

Several of Istanbul's top fish restaurants are located some way from either Old City or Beyoğlu, so that for the visitor to them there for lunch or dinner has the faint air of making a pilgrimage. If you make the trek up to Poseidon, nestling in the affluent locale of Bebek, any doubt about whether the journey was worth it will be quickly smoothed away by maître d' Mehmet Kahraman, who handles his customers – ranging from in-the-know tourists to Turkish celebrities – with considerable charm. The outdoor terrace, which almost hangs over the Bosphorus, will impress just as much, and last, but certainly not least, is the fish, super fresh, as one would expect, and prepared with con-summate skill. A superb restaurant. Book in advance.

Food 8, Service 9, Atmosphere 8

Refik, Sofayali Sokak 10–12, Asmalımescit
Tel: 0212 243 2834
Open: midday–3pm, 6pm–midnight. Closed Saturday lunch
and Sundays.   65 YTL

Refik opened in 1954 and is owned by Refik Arslan. It is one of
the most famous *meyhanes* in town (and you should visit at least
one while in Istanbul), offering the classic combination of *meze*
and *rakı*. It has long attracted a loyal following among Istanbul's
political intellectuals and is apparently full of lefties, the kind of
people who know how to talk. Unfortunately, ignorance of
Turkish may leave you oblivious to their incisive comments on
dialectic materialism and the relationship between Kemalism and
Socialism. Nevertheless, when you dine at Refik you're dropping
in on a real local scene, especially in winter, when you're confined to the simple but smart interior, decorated with myriad
photos, and everything feels intimate and convivial. In summer,
Refik's tables join the general, lively eating free-for-all that has
now colonized the entirety of Sofayali Sokak, a state of affairs for
which Refik's popularity has been largely responsible. The food's
top quality – try the *arnavut cigeri* (calf's liver); if you want to try
the *meze* dishes you select them by pointing at them in glass-
fronted fridges. So at least the language barrier won't get in the
way of your stomach.

Food 8, Service 8, Atmosphere 8

**Seasons Restaurant, Four Seasons Hotel,
Tevfikhane Sokak 1, Sultanahmet**
Tel: 0212 638 8200
Open: midday–3pm, 7–11pm daily   120 YTL

One of the finest (mostly) European restaurants in Istanbul
belongs to the Four Seasons in Sultanahmet. The setting is an
elegant conservatory and beautiful courtyard, which errs on
the tasteful side of opulence (except for the piped in music).
The menu changes every season, adapting to the best of
what's locally available, but dishes are generally adorned with
touches of French finery, Italian classicism and the odd nod
to the Far East. Regulars also include dishes such as grilled
sea bass, perfectly done. The Sunday brunch is legendary and
should be experienced. Pricey by Istanbul standards, it's a
lavish affair that should set you up for a great siesta.

Food 9, Service 8, Atmosphere 7

**Sunset Grill & Bar, Yol Sokak 1, off Adnan Saygun
Caddesi, Ulus Parkı, Ulus**
Tel: 0212 287 0357
Open: midday–3pm, 7pm–2am daily   110 YTL

A touch of California on the Bosphorus, Sunset's been open for
more than a decade and the fact that it's still buzzing, popular

with the smart crowd and winning awards, confirms its quality. Set in the leafy and arboreal surrounding of Ulus Park, on a hill overlooking the Bosphorus, it has a stunning location (though is a fair taxi ride from wherever you're likely to be), which it makes great use of with its lovely terrace, replete with modern, wave-shaped awnings. The food hails from three continents (Europe, Asia and America, so is a general fusion), seasoned with the contents of the restaurant's own herb garden. The sushi is the best in town, while the Turkish menu changes daily depending on what fantastic ingredients they can get their hands on; the 'Californian' cuisine dishes are well done. Add one of Turkey's best wine cellars and you've got a fine, cool restaurant – an excellent dinner destination, from where you'll enjoy the myriad twinkling lights adorning the Bosphorus shores, which, if you squint hard and drink a bit, almost look like stars…

Food 7, Service 7, Atmosphere 8

Ulus 29, Kireçhane Sokak 1, Adnan Saygun Caddesi, Ulus Parkı, Ulus
Tel: 0212 265 6181
Open: midday–4pm, 7pm–midnight daily   100 YTL

Located just above the swish Sunset Grill on the same hill is the similarly glamorous Ulus 29, with (again) fantastic views of the Bosphorus enjoyed from a lovely semi-circular terrace. Owned by lifestyle entrepreneur Metin Fadillioglu and his interior designer wife Zeynep, the restaurant is smartly decorated and perennially popular. The '29' bit of the name refers to 29 classic dishes on the menu – Turkish and around the Eastern Med – all well prepared. Alternatively you can have a spot of sushi, which seems oddly popular on this particular hill in Ulus (taking advantage perhaps of a secret local source of sushi chefs). The bar is notable, serving a good range of cocktails, making Ulus 29 all in all a great restaurant, well worth the trip.

Food 7, Service 7, Atmosphere 8

Vogue, Spor Caddesi 92, BJK Plaza A Blok 13, Akaretler, Beşiktaş
Tel: 0212 227 2545
Open: 10.30am–3pm, 7pm–midnight daily   90 YTL

Arriving in the courtyard between a rash of anonymous office blocks is an unpromising start to this dining experience, but an assorted array of greeters, door-openers and ushers whisk you into a lift, which soon deposits you on the building's top floor and in another world, which lives up to its name. TV screens set into the slick, wood-panelled walls play Fashion TV non-stop, with long-legged beauties endlessly striding back and forth. The waiting staff aren't bad, either (though generally a tad shorter than their on-screen versions). Better still is the amazing view.

The food meanwhile is the typical international mix now de rigueur in restaurants that cater for wealthy 'cool seekers' (to use a revolting phrase I recently read in an American magazine) who take menus with multiple-personality disorders as signifiers

of social sophistication. Sushi, salads, European classics and south-east Asian dishes sit side by side, mostly well done. The wine list is particularly extensive, as is the cigar selection, so, if you want to puff on a fat one, Vogue's the place. Sunday brunch here is popular and recommended if you don't make it in the evening.

Food 7, Service 8, Atmosphere 8

Wan-na, Meşrutiyet Caddesi 151, Tepebaşı
Tel: 0212 243 1794 www.istanbuldoors.com
Open: 7pm–midnight daily. Closed July–September.   85 YTL

The asymmetric lighting-display-cum-sculpture in the entrance, authored by one Mahmut Antar just in case you want to order your own domestic version, screams out: 'We are hip and cool so bring your wallet.' Inside, sleek lines of dark wood tables, lit by more asymmetric lighting units, stretch into the distant back room, while immediately before you is the spatially challenged bar, which must count as one of the most glamorous corridors in the city, being tightly packed with most of Istanbul's attractive smart set. The cocktails here have heritage, their secrets passed on by Nam Long restaurant in London, known above all for its

'Flaming Ferrari' cocktail, emblematic, for the British anyway, of the greedy 1980s. One fears that its inclusion here is not mitigated by any sarcastic retro intent (any rapacious traders reading this who have a fit of nostalgia may want to head to Wan-na straight away). The chefs too have pedigree, trained in some of the top south-east Asian restaurants in Sydney (more impressive

than it sounds). In any case Wan-na's Vietnamese, Thai, Chinese and Japanese dishes are delicious and stylishly presented. Not open in the high summer season.

Food 8, Service 7, Atmosphere 8

Yakup 2, Asmalımescit Caddesi 35–37, Tünel
Tel: 0212 249 2925
Open: midday–2am daily   60 YTL

Misty-eyed Beyoğlu old-timers will tell you that in days gone by *meyhanes* like Refik used to be so cheap that no one would bother cooking at home or buying the groceries and instead dine there most evenings, giving the place a cosy community feeling. Now that Asmalımescit, once a haunt of pimps, ladies (and trannies) of the night and assorted bohemian types, has been hauled up a notch or two, everything's got a little more refined and foreigners have started dropping in, messing up the local ambience (but lengthening till receipts). Yakup 2, a *meyhane* owned by Yakup Arslan, brother of Refik, round the corner from

Sofayali Sokak, retains a little more of the old, earthy feel, which basically stems from having slightly less starched linen about the place. Surviving local bohemians, well known for their dislike of starched linen, accordingly frequent the place, using the excuse of eating prodigious quantities of the excellent *meze* for drinking even more impressive quantities of *rakı*.

Food 8, Service 7, Atmosphere 8

Hg2 Istanbul

drink...

Long before they were Muslims the Turks were drinkers. Old habits die hard, or, in this particular case, not at all and instead flourished and grew, helped along by the Ottomans' imaginatively liberal interpretation of religious strictures that have had a rather more sobering effect in many lands further east. Indeed the hobby of extreme and sustained drinking was given the imperial imprimatur by a catalogue of inebriated sultans, such as Mahmut II, who managed to die of alcohol poisoning in 1839.

However the habit wasn't adopted by the more God-fearing masses and consequently this is not the land of one-thousand-and-one drinks, but three: *rakı*, beer and wine. *Rakı*, the national drink, is made from fermented grapes infused with aniseed and is similar to French *pastis*. Drunk with water or ice (only barbarians take it neat) it is the essential companion to *meze*. Efes, is the refreshing, and suspiciously ubiquitous, leading Turkish beer (its marketing manager is clearly a dangerous megalomaniac – on many streets every shop hoarding and canopy is dedicated to Efes). Turkish wine, not a phrase that typically inspires confidence, is improving and becoming more popular at home and abroad. Its relative cheapness helps. Doluca and Kavaklıdere are the two main wine makers. The latter has the best offerings – Çankaya its top white, Dikmen its premium red. There is also a range of indigenously fermented spirits, vodka, gin and so on, which should be approached cautiously, if at all. Imported spirits pay a hefty surcharge that has sadly stunted the growth of a cocktail culture.

When it comes to drinking venues, however, Istanbul has an abundance of choice, including some of the most spectacular bars imaginable thanks to the city's wealth of outstanding views and vistas. Geographically they are concentrated in Beyoğlu and in hotspots along the European Bosphorus shore such as Oratköy and Kuruçeşme, with few notable options in Sultanahmet or on the Asian side. It's also worth pointing out that many of the places separated here into the Drink, Eat, Party and Snack sections are in fact places where you can do all four (perhaps even all at once).

Around sunset on a summer's day there are few places better than sleekly modern Nu Terras, located on the seventh floor of a block in Pera, perfectly aligned as it is with the setting sun. Stunning panoramic views are also the raison d'être for 360° (see Party), Leb-i-Derya and Vogue (see Eat), all crisply contemporary and all popular with Istanbul's fashionable crowd.

A different cool crowd, younger, creative types with slightly less cash, frequent Cihangir favourites Smyrna and Leyla (see Snack), and Kino in Asmalımescit.

Bars such as Badehane, in Asmalımescit, offer a simpler and more raucous atmosphere. Meanwhile the many indistinguishable Galata Bridge bars, though tacky, present beautiful views of the Bosphorus if you're looking in the right direction (away from the bridge), especially at dusk (and they have pool tables).

For a contrast with all of the above and a hint of Old Stamboul try the elegant K.V., with its tasteful mix of the Viennese and Parisian styles that once gave Pera its dash, or the wonderfully eccentric bar at the fading Büyük Londra Hotel, which combines the varied charms of caged parrots, Victorian décor, Ottoman chandeliers and slightly incompetent (but bow-tied) staff.

In Sultanahmet the Yeşil Ev Beer Garden is a rare, leafy, oasis and the perfect place to recuperate after sightseeing, though with the domes and minarets of the Hagia Sophia and Blue Mosque flanking the hotel you can keep looking if you want to.

5 Kat, Soğancı Sokak 7, Taksim
Tel: 0212 293 3774 www.5kat.com
Open: 10am–2am daily

Velvety. In any other city this would be rendezvous central for
high-class Goths. Owned and run by Turkish actress Yasemin
Alkaya, star of independent Turkish movies such as *Woman*

Smelling a Candle and *Woman Without a Roof* (the titles lose
something in the translation), the fifth-floor bar ('kat' meaning
floor) is decked out with heavy, plush furniture and velvet
drapes, all in dark, seductive colours, making it a good, if
extremely camp, location for a winter's drink (or bite to eat). In
summer when heavy velvet becomes a little too outré even for 5
Kat regulars (assorted creative types), the action moves upstairs
to the lovely roof terrace, with, needless to say, excellent views
of the surrounding city. Even in the sunshine, though, touches of
kitsch survive, with a string of those brightly coloured, swirly,
plastic things that you can get in hippy-dippy shops decorating
the bar. It's worth the journey to the slightly out-of-the-way (but
only slightly) street off Sıraselviler Caddesi.

Badehane, General Yazgan Sokak 5, Tünel
Tel: 0212 249 0550
Open: 9am–2am daily

It's not much to look at when it's empty, being a small, single room just off Sofayalı Sokak with the simplest furniture and a non-existent rather than minimal colour scheme. But when it gets into full swing it certainly grabs hold of one's attention, attracting as it does a young crowd, mainly in their 20s, liable to

break into spontaneous and raucous dancing. If you like your drinks and entertainment simple, fun and unpretentious Badehane is a good choice. Since it's located in the heart of lively Asmalımescit you can have plenty of other options to head to afterwards. The place retains a memory of its original intention, to be a healthy eaterie, in the form of the nice food served up by owner, Madame Bade.

Bebek Hotel, Cevdet Pafla Caddesi 34, Bebek
Tel: 0212 358 2000 www.bebekhotel.com.tr
Open: midday–1am daily

If you make it all the way up the Bosphorus to Bebek, make sure you stop for a coffee or a drink at the Bebek Hotel's wonderful bar, located on a veranda that hovers over the edge of the Bosphorus. The surrounding, pretty, waterside houses and myriad moored yachts make for an idyllic scene, especially on a sunny spring or summer's day. The last word in Istanbulli elegance, the bar has been attracting the glamorous and well-heeled, older set from the exclusive suburbs of north Istanbul for decades. While you're in Bebek don't forget to go and get some of the world's best marzipan from Bebek Badem Ezmecsi, just down the road.

Beyoğlu Pub, Halep Pasajı, İstiklal Caddesi 140, Beyoğlu
Tel: 0212 252 3842
Open: midday-2am daily

A strange bar, in a strange place, the Beyoğlu Pub attracts a
close-knit, insider crowd of middle-aged, professional Istanbullis
who gossip and talk business late into the night on its expansive
terrace (which, almost uniquely, doesn't have a good view of
anything – perhaps that's why its popular) or in its reasonably

well-designed interior (dark wood, cream furniture). It's a good
place to avoid other tourists, especially since it's hidden away on
the first floor of a run-down shopping arcade, Halep Pasajı, on
İstiklal Caddesi.

Büyük Londra Hotel, Meflrutiyet Caddesi 117, Tepebaşı
Tel: 0212 245 0670
Open: 24 hours daily

For an antidote to the slick modernity of Istanbul's flock of fashionable new bars head to the wonderfully eccentric bar of the Büyük Londra Hotel, in which parrots are only one of the many aesthetic attractions, the other being the wonderfully OTT Victorian-period interior design and the curios dotted around. The place is likely to be fairly empty but can, randomly, be quite busy. However, the staff are commendably relaxed and unlikely to

mind if you started an enormous party of your own. The other major benefit of the Büyük Londra's bar is its promise of 24-hour drinking, though if you do stay for the full 24 hours it would only be polite if you were to book a room.

Dulcinea, Meflelik Sokak 20, Beyoğlu
Tel: 0212 245 1071 www.dulcinea.org
Open: 10am–2am (4am Fri/Sat) daily

A bastion of urban style and immensely popular with the soft trainers brigade in their 20s and 30s, Dulcinea is a sleek, cool, long room, full of smooth, light-coloured surfaces, tasteful furniture and fittings and projected artworks. DJs and a lively events programme provide life, energy and noise (especially in the downstairs performance space) while a Mediterranean kitchen sustains the crowd with breakfast, lunch and dinner. Or at least that's what it was like. Undergoing renovations at the time of writing, Dulcinea promises to reopen in winter 2005 with its winning style refreshed.

Galata Bridge Bars, Galata Bridge
Open: various times but generally close around 2am

If the repellently squat form of the new Galata Bridge has a redeeming feature it's the bars along either side of its mezzanine level. I say if because the Galata Bridge bars are not to everyone's taste, being loud and tacky. However, if you want an uncomplicated beer, a game of pool and a good spot from which to watch dusk fall on the city then they're a good bet (the pool is optional, by the way). Then, if you like fish and want to keep up

the rough-and-ready tone for the evening, you can stroll to the small cooking establishments behind Galata's fish market (on the Galata side of the Golden Horn and to the left as you walk towards Galata) and get yourself some lovely fresh, grilled fish.

Gizil Bahçe, Nevizade Sokak 27, Beyoğlu
Tel: 0212 249 2192
Open: midday–2am daily

It's called Gizil Bahçe, 'secret garden', for a reason. Without any sign at its entrance it's difficult to find. In winter when the streets are empty you wouldn't know a bar was there at all, while in summer it's hard to differentiate Gizil Bahçe's crowd from the general melee on Nevizarde Sokak. Cunningly, our photo will enable you to subvert its attempt at cool, exclusive anonymity. Inside one finds a young (sometimes quite studenty), trendy (and trying-a-little-too-hard-to-be-trendy) crowd, nursing beers, posing and (probably) pontificating about popular culture.

The deliberate gloominess and carefully chosen, non-matching bits of scruffy furniture cement the youthful, creative atmosphere.

Isis, Kadife Sokak 26, Kadiköy
Tel: 0216 349 7381   www.isis.com.tr.tc
Open: 11am–2am daily

Set on Kadiköy's prime street for intoxication, Kadife Sokak, Isis is a bar-cum-dance venue in an old three-storey house. The Egyptian theme sets the visual tone with murals and statuary but happily doesn't spill over into the programming of the live music. The lovely, large patio-cum-garden at the back, with tiled and wooden flooring, has a distinctly medieval feel about it, with cast-iron braziers attached to the stone walls, and its arrangement of the two rows of seating against the walls, so that they almost ceremonially face each other. The luridly coloured cocktails, however, quickly dispel any sense of temporal dislocation, as only modern drinks could look so toxic. They are however inexplicably popular with those in their 20s and 30s who frequent Isis.

The James Joyce, Balo Sokak 26, Beyoğlu
Tel: 0212 244 7970   www.theirishcentre.com
Open: 3pm–2am daily

At the time of writing, the James Joyce, Istanbul's only Irish pub, scandalously serves neither Guinness nor any other kind of porter or stout. Despite this serious flaw the surprisingly enormous establishment located opposite the bottom of Nevizarde Sokak is popular with the full variety of English-speaking ex-pats and locals. Other Irish clichés are on display, though, including fading posters of James Joyce's Dublin and portraits of Oscar Wilde (who, I firmly believe, would have hated the place). Snobs like Wilde aside, it's fun, obviously casual and occupies a very

pretty building (the pub's unexpected library is very nice –
though low on books). And if you suddenly become bored with
Turkish culture you can take advantage of the pub's raft of

regular Irish activities including Irish music sessions, the Irish film
club meeting and salsa dancing.

 K.V., Tünel Geçidi 10, Asmalımescit
Tel: 0212 251 4338
Open: 8am–2am daily

At the bottom Sofayalı Sokak you can find a glimpse of Old
Constantinople in the form of Hace Gündoğdu's restaurant and
bar, K.V. A decorative, wrought-iron gate opens onto a passage
filled with tables interspersed with tall, abundant plants, an area

that is especially beautiful at night when it is subtly and quite magically lit. Inside the old 19th-century building Gündoğdu, who owns the next-door antique shop Artrium, has decorated the rooms to recall the Viennese and Parisian styles once so common in the area. Cabinets full of antique bottles, old 19th-century fans, odd examples of Victorian clothing, ancient telephones and other curiosities conjure a comforting nostalgic air, which means that K.V. is as enchanting in winter as it is in summer. Happily, despite the historical touches, K.V. attracts a mixed bag of locals more than tourists.

Kays, Güneflli Sokak 32, Cihangir, Beyoğlu
Tel: 0212 249 5424
Open: 11am–1am daily

After a spell working and living in Germany, Kay's charming owner came back to Istanbul and decided to set up a bar with a menu reflecting his (odd) liking for northern European food. If you're missing your schnitzels or your bratwurst, then you must run to Kay's as quickly as you can to reserve your table. The place is very popular with various brands of European ex-pats and was something of a comfort zone for the British ex-pat community after the lethal bomb attack on the British Consulate in 2002. Young Turks from trendy Cihangir also like the place, possibly because it doesn't try too hard to be cool, but is instead small, relaxed and informal, with a pleasant, simple wood décor.

You can eat or just drink, as you wish.

Kino, Sofayalı Sokak 4, Asmalımescit
Tel: 0212 245 0010
Open: midday–midnight. Closed Sundays.

The provocatively voluptuous cartoon female character painted onto the sign by the entrance is sadly misleading as one is hard pressed to find any Lara Croft types inside. Not that the girls here aren't attractive, it's just that they're more likely to be wielding a paintbrush, a tape recorder or something else creative-industries related than wearing hot pants and brandishing a loaded weapon. Aside from that disappointment Kino is a lovely little bar in the middle of the Asmalımescit hotspot, pulling in a fashionable crowd, generally in their mid 20s and 30s. Its interior is tiny, decorated with painted murals and retro-patterned furniture; outside meanwhile is a smallish but lovely garden that is extremely popular on warm evenings.

Leb-i-Derya, Kumbaracı Yokuflu Kumbaracı Han 115–117, Beyoğlu
Tel: 0212 293 4989
Open: 5pm–4am daily

The main attraction for the smart Istanbul set who frequent Leb-i-Derya is themselves. By rights, though, it should be the views. On the top floor of a tall, early 20th-century building just off İstiklal Caddesi, Leb-i-Derya was recently renovated after a destructive fire. The new décor is straightforwardly light and contemporary, preferring to let your attention be taken up with the vistas. The cocktails served by the very friendly staff are pretty good and strangely seem to get better as the evening wears on, peaking in the very small hours. Food is also served and plenty of people come here to dine, but it's not the best and if you do eat here then order something simple and not Turkish, which is done better elsewhere.

Nu Terras, Meflrutiyet Caddesi 145–147, Tepebaflı
Tel: 0212 245 6070
Open: 6.30pm–2am (4am Fri/Sat) daily. Closed Oct–May.

Around sunset in summer there are few places more (literally) dazzlingly spectacular to have a drink than Nu Terras, a smooth, ultra-cool bar atop an elegant seven-storey, 19th-century building in Pera. As if designed with an astronomical precision that would put the architects of Stonehenge to shame (the owners probably just struck lucky), Nu Terras is perfectly aligned with the setting sun so that as it falls it spills out, reflecting on the sleek, smoked glass bar and the shiny tabletops. Accordingly it's one of the few places where sunglasses are actually a medical necessity rather than a fashion faux pas. DJs spin away as you sip your cocktails and watch Istanbul's beautiful crowd file in. Nu Terras is more than a bar, though, being the summer berth for the very good and very smart Lokanata restaurant on the building's ground floor (which is shut during summer) and serving a similar menu, making it hard to leave, even after the sun goes down.

Pia, Bekar Sokak 6, off İstiklal Caddesi, Beyoğlu
Tel: 0212 252 7100
Open: 3pm–2am daily

Though small, Pia, just of the Taksim end of İstiklal, manages to exude a good deal of atmosphere. It attracts a regular and select crowd of locals as well as its fair share of passing tourists drawn in by its warm, wood-panelled walls and ornate mirrors. Pia has a reputation for being frequented by attractive women, promulgated by previous guidebooks, which counterproductively

encourages solitary, male foreigners to flock to the bar and scare
off the aforementioned attractive women. You must therefore
discourage such rumours even if you happen to find them to be
true.

Soho Terras, İstiklal Caddesi 365, Floor 7, Beyoğlu
Tel: 0212 245 7782 www.sohoistanbul.com
Open: 10pm–2am daily

Seven storeys above İstiklal Caddesi and the tacky Beyoğlu is
Merkezi shopping centre, through which you have to go to reach
it, Soho Terras is a contemporary, cool-cum-kitsch destination
that is one of the most popular bars in the centre of town. The
brightly coloured chairs and sofas are almost as loud as the top
DJs who come here to play their electronica and trance tunes,
but not quite. Whether it's the sofas or the music is uncertain,
but the city's hip, young 20s and 30s crowd love the place. The
Soho Terras has also has a 'gay section' in the corner, called
G-Launch, a potentially divisive move that, nevertheless, makes
the Soho Terras one of the first 'mixed' venues in town.

Sultan Pub, Divan Yolu 2, Sultanahmet
Tel: 0212 528 1719
Open: 8am–2am daily

Sultanahmet is not blessed with a profusion of elegant or even pleasant bars. So unless you want to relive your backpacking days, in which case there is plenty of choice, the Sultan Pub, among a few others, will have to do. Suffering something of a multi-personality disorder the Sultan Pub has a nice European-café-style spread of tables while inside on the ground floor is an American-style bar, with slatted blinds and neon signs. Upstairs on the roof terrace, with – yes – lovely views of the historic old city, the Sultan Pub suddenly breaks into sleek modernity, with expensive looking 'design features' dotted around and minimalist furniture. Despite the over-design the upstairs is the nicest place for a drink.

Taps, Atiye Sokak 5, Teflvikiye
Tel: 0212 296 2020 www.tapsistanbul.com
Open: 11.30am–1am Sun–Thu, 11.30am–2am Fri–Sat

Istanbul's first micro-brewery is about the only place in town to go if you're a beer fanatic and have developed a dislike for the ubiquitous Efes pilsener. Just FYI they brew four (tasty) beers: Kolsch, Red Ale, Stout and a Strong Ale. Located in the smart district of Teflvikiye it appeals to a youthful, upmarket crowd eager to fill the trendiest venues possible. Taps, happy to recipro-cate, signals its fashionability with lots of stainless steel, exposed ventilation systems and glaring and loud TVs. The relationship is consummated for both parties over the relatively pricey food and drink. Still, clearly someone's doing something right as the place is packed most of the time.

Urban, Kartal Sokak 6 (off İstiklal Caddesi), Beyoğlu
Tel: 0212 252 1325
Open: 11am–1am daily

A particularly nice café-cum-bar that in good Istanbul fashion
serves decent food as well. Its interior has an attractive Parisian
feel to it, perfect for a lazy breakfast or afternoon coffee lingering over the paper, while outside a small terrace-like set-up of
tables is shaded by leafy creepers that climb over the iron
climbing frame. A popular venue with slightly older sophisticated
media and cultural types, Urban is often used as a starting-point
for an evening's adventure. The especially nice staff deserve a
mention.

Yeşil Ev Beer Garden, Kabasakal Caddesi 5, Sultanahmet
Tel: 0212 517 6785
Open: 10.20am–11pm daily

A more elegant option than the Sultan Pub, the bucolic Yeşil Ev Beer Garden is lovelier also than the decent hotel it's attached to and one of the few places in Sultanahmet that one can recommend as a good place for a drink. An ornate fountain burbles away in the centre of the stone-flagged garden, which is presently shaded by a number of tall, mature trees, an endangered species in central Istanbul. The wrought-iron garden furniture, matching streetlamps and formal staff give the place a turn-of-the-last- century ambience. The garden is just as nice for a daytime tea or coffee as it is for a long drink after a hard day's sightseeing in the Old City.

snack...

There are few cities where the street food is as cheap, plentiful or as good as here. Hawkers with their mobile units sell boiled or grilled corn-on-the-cob and rice-stuffed mussels all over town. In most areas you don't have to go far to find a *kebabçi* or *köftecisi*, where the traditional and uncomplicated fare of a plate of *köfte* (spiced, grilled meatballs) is served with side orders of rice, salad and *ayran*, the yoghurt drink of which Turks are so fond. Try Tarihi Selim Usta Sultanahmet Köftecisi on Divan Yolu in the heart of Sultanahmet, or Arnavut Köfte in Balat, both in the Old City, or indeed the countless, nameless others, avoiding the more obviously touristy joints in picture postcard areas, where the relationship between the cook and his art is loveless, dictated by money, expediency and circumstance.

Low cholesterol and high omega-3 counts, meanwhile, will be the reward of those who stick around the city's fishy areas – Kumkapı, in the south of the old city, or near Galata Bridge – and consume their freshly grilled fish sandwiches.

Other traditional pleasures are to be found at Vefa Bozacısı, near the Grand Bazaar, which serves up *boza* in winter, a nourishing, fermented millet drink, unchanged since Turkic pre-history, and *şira*, fermented grape juice. Also indigenous is the *nargile*, or hookah. Of course smoking a 'hubbly bubbly' is

considered to be the height of hippie naffness in the West, and for most of the 20th century a self-respecting Turk would have agreed, bracketing it along with fez-wearing in the highest category of cultural no-nos. Now the *nargile* has made a come-back. Visit the *nargile* cafés in Tophane or even Erenler Çay Bahçesi, next door to the Grand Bazaar, and you'll find more locals than visitors.

An altogether different world is on view at the many fashionable cafés that pepper the smart and wealthy areas of Nişantışı and the Bosphorus villages. At Beyman Brasserie and Caffe Armani in Nişantışı swap your thick Turkish coffees for espressos and a feigned air of boredom. A younger, but similarly well-heeled crowd flock to the cafés in and around Oratköy, with Aşşk Café and the newly opened Housecafé (which has sisters in Azmalımescit and Nişantışı), both on the Bosphorus shoreline and especially popular.

Back in the more arty areas of Beyoğlu there is a different feel again. The Alti Café and Symrna are local hotspots in Cihangir that happily offer good food and drink all day long, with Alti particularly good on breakfasts. The nearby Miss Pizza, meanwhile, bakes the best pizzas in town. In Azmalımescit, Şimdi offers strong Italian coffee and a varied menu. Around the corner on İstiklal Caddesi, Markiz Café, with its gorgeous Art Nouveau tiled panels depicting the seasons, is a reminder of Beyoğlu's chic, cosmopolitan past. So too is the Pera Palace, where the cakes in the famous café are rather better than its rooms.

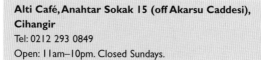

Alti Café, Anahtar Sokak 15 (off Akarsu Caddesi), Cihangir
Tel: 0212 293 0849
Open: 11am–10pm. Closed Sundays.

Run by two attractive, young Turkish ladies, the small but perfectly formed Alti Café is one of Cihangir's top spots. Its Turkish breakfasts (olives, cheese, honey, and so on) are especially popular with the area's creative types (artists, photographers,

advertising execs) though it serves food, good coffee and a full range of alcoholic beverages all day long. During spring and summer customers hang out in the cute, leafy back garden, which is full of brightly coloured throws and cushions. If you're planning to spend some time wandering around the nearby antique district of Çukurcuma (recommended) then this is an ideal place to start or finish. The prettily decorated Alti also doubles as a boutique selling Indian-style clothes designed by the owners, just to prove how naturally creative everyone around here is.

Armani Caffe, Maçka Palas, Maçka Caddesi 35, Teşvikiye
Tel: 0212 224 4477
Open: 10am–midnight daily

The districts of Nişantaşı and Teşvikiye are unashamedly concerned with style, labels and beautiful people, so if you're in the area why not head straight to its spiritual home, the Armani

Caffe? The food is stylish and beautifully presented, as are the staff and the customers. You can stop in for just a coffee, snack or light lunch. If you want something more substantial and you've remembered your wallet head upstairs to the fabulously expensive restaurant that occupies a lovely terrace.

Arnavut Köfte, Mürselpaşa Caddesi 155, Köprubaşi, Balat
Tel: 0212 531 6652
Open: 6.30am–4pm daily

Ali Iştay's small, simple, anonymous *köfte* joint in Balat is only a short taxi ride away from the Egyptian Bazaar. Like the gloriously named Tarihi Selim Usta Sultanahmet Köftecisi on Divan Yolu in

Sultanahmet it's an excellent representative of Istanbul's raft of, generally, good-quality *kebabçi* and *köftecisi*, purveyors of essential Turkish fast food, which is the staple diet of the working man. At Arnavut Köfte the lamb meatballs are tender, best accompanied with a glass of *ayran*. It is a place full of local flavour, as they say.

Aşşk Café, Muallim Naci Caddesi 170, Kuruçeşme
Tel: 0212 265 4734
Open: 9am–7.30pm (1am Apr–Oct). Closed Mondays.

A hang-out where the trendy and beautiful go to work on their melanomas, Aşşk Café is a cutely styled café on the glitzy club and bar Bosphorus strip of Kuruçeşme. Models, footballers and

everyone else who aspires to those archetypes pass the time of day over espressos. You can't fault their choice of venue. Despite being hidden behind a supermarket, Aşşk (meaning love) is superbly located right on the waterfront and benefits from a sprinkling of shade-giving trees, making it positively idyllic on a sunny day. Though a destination in itself, at night it becomes a good place to go for a drink before trying all the nearby clubs. And if at any point you feel dissatisfied with your experience (or feel the need for pasta) you can always just push past the shrubbery that separates Aşşk from the lovely Italian restaurant Mia Mensa next door and settle down for a meal.

Bambi, Sıraselviler Caddesi 20 (among others), Taksim
Tel: 0212 252 8713
Open: 24 hours daily

Back home when you get drunk and end up eating that near-
fatal, anonymous, kebab after a night out you know that there
will be no excuses good enough to assuage the guilt and shame

that will inevitably accompany the next day's painfully sober
dawn. Here at least you can docket the event as an authentic
cultural experience, especially if you head to fast-food outlet
Bambi on the corner of Taksim Square, which is something of an
Istanbulli institution, having served its kebabs 24 hours a day
since 1974. The café's popularity is clearly demonstrated by its
extraordinary and slightly sinister expansion down Sıraselviler
Caddesi, occupying as it does a string of shopfronts. Providing
excellent material for field research in anthropological studies on
intoxicated Turks (if you're lucky a fight might break out), a trip
to Bambi also offers cheap, fast and reliable kebabs.

Beymen Brasserie, Abdi İpekçi Caddesi 23/1, Maçka
Tel: 0212 343 0442
Open: 10am–midnight daily

Vying with Armani Caffe for the best place in Istanbul to look
elegant in, the smooth brasserie located on the ground floor of

Beymen's latest and slickest store also serves a commendable coffee and has an extensive menu, proving that, despite evidence

to the contrary, the store's beautiful customers don't survive on light and expensive products alone. Big windows allow everyone to be seen. It's not cheap, but nor is the company.

Café di Dolce, Kuruçeşeme Caddesi 25, Kuruçeşeme
Tel: 0212 257 7299
Open: 9am–7pm. Closed Sundays.

If you fancy a good cake and you're somewhere in the Bosphorus vicinity, then having the afternoon tea service (available throughout the day and night) at Café di Dolce is a must. In

the tiny, pretty, green, brown and beige café owner and cake-master Nilgün Ertuğ struts his stuff before your very eyes, baking as he serves. Charm your companion with one of Nilgün's distinctive heart or shooting-star-shaped biscuits. If you're alone why not buy one for the person sitting next you? The fig muffins are also highly recommended.

Carnival, Gönül Sokak 11/13, Asmalımescit, Beyoğlu
Tel: 0212 245 7025
Open: 9am–midnight daily

A tasteful little café on a small street, more an alcove really, off İstiklal Caddesi, towards the Tünel end, Carnival is bright and light and around lunchtime its counter is packed with delicious and generally healthy fare of the pasta, salads and tortilla variety. Breakfasts are good too and this is one of the nicer places to have a break while trawling down the shopping mecca of İstiklal Caddesi.

Erenler Çay Bahçesi, Çorlulu Ali Paşa Medresesi,
Yeniçeriler Caddesi 36/28, Beyazit
Tel: 0212 528 3785
Open: 7am–midnight (3am in the summer) daily

Nargile (hookah) smoking, callow-pretentious-student-style naffness in the West, was, until recently, just lamely old-fashioned in Turkey. Now it's going through a resurgence, which means your obligatory *nargile* experience won't be as embarrassing as it would have been even a few years ago. Symptomatic of this casual movement of the fickle hand of fashion is the breakdown

of the customers at Erenler Çay Bahçesi, who, despite being right next to the Grand Bazaar, are more local that foreign. Set in an old and atmospheric courtyard of an old Ottoman seminary it's a good place to be, especially as dusk falls. Sip tea and fill up on toasted cheese sandwiches. For an even more earthy *nargile* experience try the numerous and nameless cafés that cluster together off Tophane Iskelesi behind the Nusretiye Mosque, near the Bosphorus waterfront in the southeast of Beyoğlu.

The Four Seasons, Tevkifhane Sokak 1, Sultanahmet
Tel: 0212 638 8200
Open: midday–3pm, 7–11pm daily

Once the Istanbul equivalent of high tea at the Ritz was to be had at somewhere like the Pera Palace. Now, despite the enduring charm of the Pera Palace patisserie, you're better off heading to the The Four Seasons, especially if you're in the Old City anyway. Despite the lack of a grand dining room, the afternoon tea service is as impeccable and formal as one would expect (and obviously as pricey too). Nice biscuits.

House Café, Atiye Sokak 10/1, Teşvikiye
Tel: 0212 259 2377
Open: 8am–11pm daily

The super-trendy House Café has three branches, in Oratköy, Teşvikiye and Tünel. The latter is the newest and the one you're most likely to frequent as it is in the heart of the eating and drinking pleasure zone of Asmalımescit; the Oratköy branch is a good stop if you're trawling along the Bosphorus and is near the clubs of Kuruçeşme. All three have a loyal following among Istanbul's young fashionable crowd. All the girls look immaculate and sport identical haircuts and accessories, which must make it confusing for the tanned, affluent-looking open-shirted men who hang around trying to get them drunk (best to go to Oratköy if you want to take part in this kind of thing). Everything's moder-

ately expensive by Istanbul standards (so reasonable for Europeans and Americans). The cocktails are good as is the food, which is standard cool café fare – pizzas, pastas and salads. The burger is something of a speciality and recommended. Come here for a drink, snack or a full-on meal. At evenings and week-ends in the summer the House Café in Oratköy gets especially packed so book ahead if you want to eat there. The décor in all three is minimally cool and gets top marks for demonstrating the creative use of coloured lights (especially the Tünel branch).

Kaffeehaus, Tünel Meydanı 4, Tünel
Tel: 0212 245 4028
Open: 9am–9pm daily

Cunningly located on Tünel Square so that you see its entrance as you finish the steep climb from Galata to İstiklal Caddesi, Kaffeehaus indeed offers a cool, airy and contemporary-looking place to rest your feet, sip coffee and read the papers (if you can understand Turkish). According to an unscientific survey it seems to attract foreign ex-pat writers who perhaps enjoy the non-dis-tracting (pretty bare) interior design and beautiful staff.

Leyla, Akarsu Caddesi 46, Cihangir
Tel: 0212 244 5335
Open: 8am–4am daily

Run by the owners of the superb fish restaurant Doğa Balık and located on the top floor of the same building, Leyla is a new addition to Cihangir's fast-growing list of restaurants and bars. Like most places nearby you can come here to graze lightly at any time of the day or to eat properly. An Italian menu offers very acceptable pastas and plenty of snacking options too. The smoothly decorated interior, white walls and light wood-touched off by pretty patterns of coloured glass, comes alive when the sun shines in through the extensive windows. At night the elliptical bar becomes the focal point as local trendies descend en masse.

 Limonlu Bahçe, Yeniçarşı Caddesi 98, Galatasaray
Tel: 0212 252 1094
Open: 9.30am–1am daily

After ducking and diving through a few doorways and passages off the steep slope of Yeniçarşı Caddesi, you'll find yourself in the very pleasant, big back garden that is called Limonlu Bahçe – the Lemon Garden. It's got a great, relaxed atmosphere, helped along by the comfy pillows and cushions, hammocks and casual (in every sense) staff, presenting an excellent haven from the noisy busyness of İstiklal Caddesi. A cool crowd in their 20s and 30s fills the place in the evenings and weekends, though it's generally quiet on weekdays. It's lovely for a drink, but the food, though fine, isn't the best. Gardens are pretty rare in Istanbul, and this one's particularly nice.

Mado Ice Cream, all over the city
Open: most of the time   www.mado.com.tr

With outlets all over the city Mado is Istanbul's (and Turkey's) favourite ice-cream brand and parlour chain. Its gloopy wares are made the traditional Turkish way, from goat's milk, sugar and

salep, a powder made from natural wild orchid tubers that allegedly has aphrodisiac powers, which perhaps accounts for the product's enormous popularity. There is an array of more than 80 flavours on offer including date, pomegranate, fig, carrot, pumpkin and, for that oriental touch, spiced.

Mangerie, Cevdetpaşa Caddesi 69 (3rd Floor), Bebek
Tel: 0212 263 5199
Open: 8am–10.30pm daily

A terrace floor in an old, wooden apartment building in Bebek
forms the setting for one of the loveliest café-restaurants in the
city and is the location of choice for CNN Turkey staff, who film

a regular cookery programme there. A light, white colour
scheme complements the place's period features; meanwhile you
can sit back and watch as your meal is prepared in an open
kitchen. Breakfast, lunches and dinners are all good here (and not
too formal), and you can come for a coffee and light bite and
enjoy the chic company. Note that this is one of the few places
in Istanbul that serves decent bacon, so it's worth the trip if
you're missing your porky fry-ups (which are of course provided
with extreme elegance here). The only drawback, from your
point of view, is that Mangerie is in Bebek, and you probably
aren't. After purchasing the plugged Bebek marzipan and having a
drink in the Bebek Hotel Bar, have a bite here.

Markiz Café, İstiklâl Caddesi 360, Beyoğlu
Tel: 0212 246 8394
Open: 9am–10pm daily

A survivor from the Pera's glamorous days, the Markiz was recently saved from dereliction and spruced up by the owners of the Richmond Hotel across the street. Despite the probable press of tourists you'll encounter it's worth a visit to sit and enjoy the tiled

Art Noveau wall designs of French artist J. A. Arnoux, which depict two of the seasons (summer and winter got lost somewhere along the way). The Markiz used to be stuffed with members of Istanbul's intelligentsia and artistic community who were attracted to it primarily by the pastries baked in the special pastry oven the café's original owner's brought over from Paris and by each other's sophisticated company. The pastries are still good, as are the coffees. Sadly atmosphere is rather harder to restore.

 Meşale, Arasta Bazaar 45, Sultanahmet
Tel: 0212 518 9562
Open: 24 hours daily

Occupying a corner of the Sultanahmet Mosque's complex of buildings, Meşale is a sunken café next to the Arasta Bazaar, where you can rest underneath the awnings have a *nargile*, drink and a snack. Its location makes it pretty popular with tourists, though in the evening workers from local shops and businesses come here too. There's live music most nights and occasional performances of Dervish dancing.

Miss Pizza, Akarsu Caddesi, Havyar Sokak No 7, Cihangir
Tel: 0212 251 3278
Open: 11am–11pm daily

If you get tired of the *meze*, fresh fish and so on, you can fill up on the lovely wood-oven-baked pizzas at the newly opened Miss Pizza. Run by the promoters of the über-cool Godet nighclub,

who have a big following in the Cihangir area, it's often packed and highly popular. So get here early to get your pizza. Given the owners' dab hands at manipulating styles and fashions it's hard to tell whether the joint's décor is super-subtle kitsch or just eco-nomical; either way it looks like a little slice of Italy in Istanbul, with red and white check as the dominant motif.

Nature and Peace, Büyükparmakkapi Sohak 14, Beyoğlu
Tel: 0212 245 2932
Open: midday–1am daily

Nature and Peace signals the fact that it's one of the first restaurants aimed at vegetarians in the city by sticking decorative plastic models of corn cobs and other fine vegetables on its walls.

Amusingly, however, the owners have started foraying into the world of meat, presumably because vegetarians are so rare a species here. Nevertheless the family-run eatery has a good, healthy menu – full pulses, rice and beans – as well as good dessert options, all served in a modestly decorated environment (plastic fruit and veg are inherently modest). If you go in the evening you can always head over the street to Şal, for a taste of wild Turkish folk music, tanked up on your nutrients.

**Pera Palace Patisserie & Terrace Bar,
Meşrutiyet Caddesi 98/100, Tepebaşi**
Tel: 0212 251 4560
Open: 8am–1am daily

Few hotels can boast the range and quality of roles in fiction that the Pera Palace has on its CV, popping up as it does in Eric Ambler's *The Mask of Demetrius*, Agatha Christie's *Murder on the Orient Express*, Ian Fleming's *From Russia with Love* and Alfred Hitchcock's *The Lady Vanishes*. Despite this and its Victorian glory you may not want to stay here (see Sleep section). But if you don't you should drop in some time on its still elegant and charmingly period patisserie for a cake and coffee, served in grand hotel style. Alternatively, if you're an alcoholic, head upstairs to the terrace bar for a cool drink. The only blot on these particular landscapes is the number of tourists you'll find there clutching, er… guide books, and spoiling the atmosphere

(so hide the book and try not to look like a tourist. Elegant late 19th-century period dress should do it.)

Pierre Loti Café, Pierre Loti Caddesi 5, Çemberlitaş
Tel: 0212 518 3174
Open: 9am–midnight

Really this entry is just an excuse for me to tell you about Pierre Loti (1850–1923, real name Julien Viand). Sadly the unabashedly romantic and Orientalist French novelist is largely forgotten, his prose being a little too purple for modern taste. Except, that is, among the Turks, who love him for the very good reason that he loved them. Here's Pierre waxing lyrical about Istanbul in his novel *Les Désenchantées*: 'As he felt deeply Turkish on this warm, clear evening… on the familiar esplanade in front of the Syulatn-Fatih's mosque. He wanted to dream there, in the pure cool of the evening, and in the sweet Oriental peace, smoking hookahs while surrounded by dying splendour, decay, religious silence and prayer.' As for the Pierre Loti café, it is very old and situated northwest of the Old City at the top of a leafy hill above the Eyüp Sultan Cemetery, with a beautiful view over the Golden

Horn and the city's skyline. The management tentatively suggests that it might have been this café that Loti visited while staying in Eyüp in 1876. This is exactly the sort of thing medieval monks used to say about their saint's relics, hoping to draw in the

punters while knowing very well that their holy bones belonged to a sheep who died of the plague a few decades earlier. Nevertheless, it's a quiet, calm, bucolic place of which Loti would have approved (but he would have hated the modern development, also called Pierre Loti, where your taxi will drop you off – head down the gravel path to the old tearoom).

The Pudding Shop, Divan Yolu 6, Sultanahmet
Tel: 0212 522 2970
Open: 7am–11pm daily

This place deserves mention for having played a starring role in the Turks' least favourite film, *Midnight Express*, which portrays the Turkish jailors, of an American caught smuggling dope, as a bunch of medieval, perverted sadists (the Turks can't stand being called medieval). It was a really hippy joint in the 1960s, a stopping-off point on the trail to India, but owners have cleverly reduced the place's ambience to zero by giving it a modern canteen-style refit and plastering the legend 'The world famous Pudding Shop' all over the place. Do watch *Midnight Express*. Don't eat here (a drink is okay). Try not to get arrested.

Şimdi, Asmalımescit Sokak 9, Tünel
Tel: 0212 252 1325
Open: 11am–1am daily

One of the better options for a coffee and a snack if you're around the Tünel end of İstiklal Caddesi is the casually elegant Şimdi with its Illy coffee, lovely modern chandelier and attractive blue tiling. On warm days the sliding doors are pulled back so that the comfortable front section with its deep, low sofas is exposed to the street. The back eating area includes a space that is effectively a courtyard, open to the sky and surrounded on all sides by the windows of the flats above. The long menu is simple (pastas, salads, sandwiches) and includes good (Turkish-style) breakfast options. There's also (notionally) a free internet termi-

nal, which suffers from frequent technical problems. If you sit at the back in the courtyard beware: residents of the flats water their plants with callous disregard for the diner below.

Smyrna, Akarsu Caddesi 29, Cihangir
Tel: 0212 244 2466
Open: 10am–midnight daily

Though only a few years old Smyrna is dead-centre for Cihangir's cool social scene. The eclectic retro tone is set at the entrance by an open wooden cupboard spilling over with a cute-

ly (though deliberately) weird collection of bric-à-brac, dolls, typewriters, old bottles and so on. The rest of the décor is similarly mixed up, with lots of comfortable old sofas and armchairs. The clientele would like to be eclectic, too, but they're all arty types (and so constitute a social monoculture, even if it's a creative one). The food and drink, served all day and into the night, is good, though priced more in line with central London than local Istanbul, (but you're paying for the cool). There's even a super comfortable tiny platform area accessible by a steep set of ladder-steps where you can have a lounge or even lie down and the relaxed staff probably won't mind if you doze off (as long as you keep ordering food and drink in your sleep).

Sugar Club Café, Sakasalim Çikmazi 7, Beyoğlu
Tel: 0212 244 1275
Open: 10.30am–midnight daily

Down a small side street off İstiklal Caddesi is the Sugar Club Café, a small, unpretentious, modernly decorated café, which is

one of the only openly gay daytime venues in the city. Serving a nice cup of coffee and food cooked up by owner-chef Murat Söğütlüoğlu, Sugar Club Café is a nice spot to seek refuge from İstiklal Caddesi and it's not fascistically gay (you don't have to be gay to go there). Fairly quiet during the day, it picks up in the evening with people spilling out and lounging about the little backstreet.

Tarihi Selim Usta Sultanahmet Köftecisi, 12 Divan Yolu, Sultanahmet
Tel: 0212 513 1438
Open: 11am–11pm daily

Despite its forbiddingly long name, which means 'Historical Sultan Ahmet Köfte restaurant' (they're proud of their 80 years of culinary service to locals and tourists alike), this *köftecisi* serves Turkish food at its simplest and is in easy reach of the sites of Sultanahmet. The diet is one that Dr Atkins would have approved of, being just lamb meatballs, dairy products (*ayran*) and fresh veg (especially the white bean salad) with few carbs in sight. The décor is basic but pleasant and the place is perennially popular (hence the 80 years). Watch the white uniformed chefs – who must surely be suffering the conceptual version of repetitive strain syndrome and desperate to get their prongs on a chicken or steak or two for variety's sake – expertly toast your meal over their open flame grills. It's also very cheap.

Tapas Bar (Venta del Toro), Galipede Caddesi 145, Galata
Tel: 0212 243 6049
Open: 11am–2am daily

Located near Galata Tower on the steep sloping road that runs from Tünel to Galata Bridge, Venta del Toro is a Spanish tapas bar in town set up by an artistic Spanish lady who liked Istanbul so much she stayed. Bright, loud, modern mosaics with matching furniture manage to provide happy ambience in summer and are warming in winter. The well-cooked food is standard tapas fare, though it is non-standard in Istanbul of course. A good, relaxed place for breakfast or a snack at some point during the day, Venta del Toro can become raucous in the evenings, drawing as it does a healthy mixture of visitors and locals eager to drink Spanish beer and see some of the flamenco dancing that occasionally takes place on the premises.

Vefa Bozacısı, Katip Çelebi Caddesi 104, Vefa
Tel: 0212 519 4922   www.vefa.com.tr
Open: 8am–midnight daily

The beautifully tiled 1930s café, one of the prettiest, most
atmospheric and well worth a visit, is not far from the bazaar
quarter in a taxi. It's primarily famous for making *boza*, a traditional fermented millet drink served up by smartly uniformed
staff from marble tubs in winter, and *şira*, a sparkling grape drink,
on sale in summer. Vefa's strong vinegar is also renowned and
you can stock up on bottles of it to take home.

party...

Unabashed hedonists, the Turks' sincere enjoyment of the pleasures of the table is equalled by their appreciation of drinking, dancing and showing off. Accordingly Istanbul's nightclub scene is both dense and varied.

At the glittering, conspicuous consumption end of the market Istanbul's clubs effortlessly match their Mediterranean rivals in St Tropez and Beirut, albeit with a less international clientele. With their own significant tranche of the super-rich the Turks haven't yet got round to importing other peoples'.

An improbably large hoarding depicting a red Porsche coupé erected over the entrance to Rainer, the city's premier super-club, sets the none-too-subtle tone for a string of clubs, including Sortie, Angelique and Crystal, which sit on the shore of the Bosphorus in Kuruçeşme, a short drive from Beyoğlu. In summer they are, for an assorted collection of moguls, Mafiosi, models, wannabe models, footballers, miscellaneously rich and curious foreigners, the place to be seen. Place, singular, since, in the spirit of a corporate marketing exercise, the glitterati tend to maximize their visibility by visiting as many clubs in one night as is humanly possible. The interchangeability of the venues is underscored by their regular attention-seeking name changes. Sited on the shoreline, the clubs afford their clients spectacular views and, for the really flashy, the chance to avoid queues by docking their yachts at their very own piers. Extraordinarily large, they tend to house a clutch of restaurants, bars and dance-floors, so that

technically you need never leave, though on a practical level that would lead to the rapid implosion of your wallet. Off-season the clubs either move to venues in town or take a tax-efficient break.

Back in town the newly opened 360°, sitting loftily above İstiklal Caddesi, is one of the cooler alternatives to the Bosphorus clubs. Babylon, in Azmalımescit, is the city's top music venue, attracting international DJs and guitar bands. More sedately the excellent Nardis Jazz Club is the best place to sample Istanbul's surprisingly thriving jazz scene.

Istanbul's attitude towards sex and sexuality is somewhat ambivalent. Turkey's metropolitan elites are proud of the country's secularity, something of a modern extension of Ottoman traditional broadmindedness that is typified in a

speech Mehmet the Conqueror delivered to his troops during their siege of Constantinople. When the usual promises of plunder and female virgins on victory proved insufficiently moving, he hastily tacked on, 'And you will have boys, too, very many and very beautiful and of noble families.' The city fell the next day. Though homophobia is far from extinct, the gay scene is active and Be Club is a reliable hotspot. There is also a small but highly visible transvestite population, who are a world and law unto themselves (and hang out in the backstreets around Taksim, if you're asking).

On the other hand vast swathes of the population, including many Anatolian migrants to Istanbul, are traditionally Islamic in their outlook. Thus there are no legal stripclubs, brothels or adult venues in the city. The red-light district is in Aksaray, a western area of the Old City settled by East European immigrants. But illicit pleasure seekers seek at their own risk. Don't be surprised if you find a larger, more muscular and threatening Eastern European in that seedy hotel room than you bargained for.

**2C Club Inn, Abdülhakhamit Caddesi 75,
Belediye Dükkanları, Taksim**
Tel: 0212 235 6197
Open: 10pm–4am (5am Fri/Sat) daily mid-July to mid-Sept;
11am–4am Wed, Fri, Sat remainder of the year

Over a decade in business under the same name means that in
the ephemeral world of Istanbul's nightclub scene 2C is the oldest club in the city. It's likely to retain that distinction for a while

yet, for it's perennially popular, packed on the weekend with the
most mixed crowd of any of the Istanbul nightclubs, bringing in
gay and straight, young and old. In the slightly rough Taksim area,
2C offers a taste of the down and dirty side of Istanbul nightlife,
but is full of energy thanks to the banging techno and house
tunes and the eclectic vibe.

**360°, İstiklal Caddesi Mısır Apartmanı,
7th and 8th Floor, Beyoğlu**
Tel: 0212 251 1042 www.360istanbul.com
Open: 7pm–3am daily

The best nightclub in Beyoğlu, offering a touch of the glitz that
you'd get at the Kuruçeşme nightclubs within a considerably

cooler setting, is the spanking new 360°, opened at the end of 2004. Set up by Englishman turned local Sashah Anton Khan, 360° occupies a spacious, totally modern, purpose-built floor

above the lovely 19th-century Mısır Building on İstiklal Caddesi. As its name hints, the club's large terrace and glass walls allow an all-round panorama of the city, with especially nice views of the Golden Horn and the lovely belfry of next-door St Antoine Church. Inside the design is coolly minimalist in foundation, with several more contemporary-cum-retro touches like the large, circular, sculptural light over the restaurant area. All of the Bosphorus super-clubs have restaurants, but 360°'s is the best, run by the ex-head chef of the Çırağan Palace, who produces a fusion of global styles. Also extensive is the bar menu, which attempts to introduce several new cocktails to Istanbul as well as fruit frappés for the sensible non-drinkers out there, all of which are enjoyed by the generally very attractive and quite approachable crowd to the sounds of progressive house.

Anjelique, Muallim Naci Cad., Salhane Sokak 10, Ortaköy
Tel: 0212 327 2844 www.istanbuldoors.com
Open: 7pm–4am daily

Mirrors are the leitmotif at Anjelique, ostensibly so that the club's terrific Bosphorus views are reflected and bounced around the place, but I think we all know it's so that neurotic Turkish TV stars can keep themselves calm throughout the evening with quick, unsubtle checks of their mascara or gelled-back hair (no gender prejudice here). Owned by the Doors Group who seem

to be on a mission to stylize the social life of Istanbul's wealthy, party crowd, and own Wanna, Vogue (see Eat) and A'jia (Sleep), Anjelique is ultra-cool in its feel, the aforementioned mirrors set against white walls and touches of purple light. The restaurant on the terrace is typically full, but the bar and dance-floors are where the action is, and get going after midnight. Grooving alongside the slender models and beefy tanned male accompaniment are plenty of Istanbul's super-rich. On which note, if you're a guy and on the pull and you are not a) a Turkish celebrity, b) an A-list international celebrity (having been on an embarrassing reality TV show once doesn't count), c) playboy heir to a billion-dollar soap/ball-bearing/hemp manufacturing empire or d) combination of the above (extra points), then lie and pretend you are. If you are a lady with amorous intent then be warned that the kind of men you find at Anjelique are exclusively interested in those traditional feminine qualities of honesty, chastity... scratch that, I'm getting my venues mixed up, that was the guys from the Ali Pasha Mosque... interested in, er, tans and a creatively minimal approach to clothing. This applies equally to Reina, Sapphire and Sortie.

'Babylon turns Istanbul On' is the slogan and while it's a little
pat, it's kind of true. Istanbul's premier live music venue, which
attracts a great mix of acts from Scandinavian ambient outfits to

African singer-songwriters, is also famed for its club nights at
which DJs belt out a similarly eclectic range of sounds: jazz,
world music, electronica, drum'n'base and house. On Thursdays
and weekend nights the large dance-floor is often packed to its
400 capacity. Life mimics art in the diversity of the friendly
crowd, stretching from groovy business types to hedonistic stu-
dents – anyone who likes loud music and dancing really. In drawing in punters from all over town to its industrial-like space
Babylon was instrumental (intentional pun) in Asmalımescit's
recent, hyper-inflation-like rise to being party-central, for which it
richly deserves credit and custom.

An Istanbul favourite, Crystal eschews the seasonality practised by its neighbours in Kuruçeşme, staying open all year round. It conjures a different flavour of exclusivity, however, by opening only at 11.30pm and deciding to not really get going till 1am or later. The diverse crowd (in their 20s to late 30s, mainly Turks but with occasional foreigners) who fill the place (capacity 800) on Thursdays and weekend nights can't all be curious insomniacs. Most are drawn by the electro and house played by Crystal's large stable of resident DJs and the relaxed fun atmosphere, which is a good deal more casual than nearby Reina and Angelique. It doesn't have their Bosphorus views, either, being on the wrong side of Muallim Naci Caddesi, but the large lounge-bar-cum-atrium into which you walk as you arrive has glass walls

and ceilings, providing an extraordinary view of the titanic, aus-terely modernist suspension bridge that looms up near the club. The cavernous back room is a big dance pit, enlivened by a retro-futuristic motif of circular patterns and a flock of mirror balls suspended from the ceiling. It's a good place for a late-night dance.

Godet, Prof. Bulent Tarcan Sokak 3, Gayrettepe
Tel: 0212 272 1160 (Surmeli Hotel)
Open: 10.30pm–4am Wed–Sat. Closed July–Sept.

Godet is an immensely popular, peripatetic nightclub, which in its almost decade-long life has graced several venues, but managed

to take its loyal, youngish with older patches, trendy and eclectic crowd with it from place to place. Currently it has taken up residence in the moderately unlikely venue of the towering but naff Surmeli Hotel, which is something of a taxi ride out of town. But there are a few advantages to its present location. The rooftop rooms present some fantastic views of the twinkling city at night. More importantly, being in the Surmeli offers the chance for everyone to enjoy the tasteless carpets and step out of the lift on their way home at 4am and run into busloads of arriving Japanese tourists. The glass lift itself is an attraction (though obviously not the main one), rising as it does through the hotel's 1980s futuristic décor. Godet is run by the diminutive and appropriately impish Minas 'Morgul', who is generally to be found on the dance-floor clutching the club's only cocktail shaker while goading his guests to dance to the cheesy pop and techno tunes.

Nu Club, Meşrutiyet Caddesi 149/1, Tepebaşi
Tel: 0212 245 6070
Open: 11pm–4am Fri–Sat. Closed June-Nov.

If it's not summer and you're in town of an evening searching for a little subterranean excitement try Nu Club. It is part of the Nu Pera building, which houses Lokanta, the excellent fusion restaurant on the ground floor (see Eat), and Nu Terras (see Snack), its summery incarnation on the seventh floor. Nu Club is small, loud and often densely packed with Lokanta/Nu Terras's smart, attractive clientele who generally range from their late 20s to their early 40s. The intimacy is all part of the attraction, especially on the dance-floor, which, though modestly proportioned is often

lively. The DJs tend to put out a mixture of house and more dancey pop hits, and there's a strong Parisian connection thanks to some of the promoters, who regularly lure Gallic trendies over to take command of the decks for a bit.

NuBlu East, Muallim Naci Caddesi 130, Kuruçeşme
Tel: 0212 265 6912
Open: midday–4am daily

Set within a larger club complex on Muallim Naci Caddesi, called

New Yorker, Nublu East is the love child of the well-regarded tenor saxophonist and producer Ilhan Erşahin, whose playing style, for the record, is influenced by John Coltrane and Joe Henderson. After the success of his first club Nubulu, set up in New York's East Village, where he also runs a record label, Erşahin thought he'd try his hand at the same thing at home. Given the musical pedigree of its owner, it's no surprise that Nubulu Est plays a sophisticated mix of groove, reggae, pop and disco. The atmosphere and crowd is more bohemian and less flashy (not difficult) than those that frequent the other clubs on the strip, but still comprises a fair number of beautiful people.

Reina, Muallim Naci Caddesi 44, Kuruçeşme
Tel: 0212 2 259 5919 www.reina.com.tr
Open: 7pm–4am daily mid-May to mid-Oct

Leila used to be king of Istanbul's nightclub hill but has now become Sortie, lost some of its brand value and so surrendered

the meritoriously glittering, fake tiara of victory to Reina. With its Bosphorus waterfront venue, its confusing array of expensive 'guest' restaurants and bars, and last, but certainly not least (and in fact first, in that it's plastered over the entrance), its enormous hoarding, touchingly depicting a red Porsche sports coupé, Reina has the all necessary attributes of leadership. It's large, expensive and enormously popular with Istanbul's celeb-party crowd. The design is plush-minimal, cream furniture, black stone small decorative fireplaces that look as if they are from British Gas's Contemporary Range. But the décor isn't really the main attraction. For the etiquette of mating rituals in expensive Istanbul clubs, see entry for Anjelique above. Finally, as with Anjelique, if you have a yacht you can avoid the front-door heavies and glide into Reina's own dockings bays (ring ahead to reserve your berth).

Safran, Rıhtım Caddesi 52/3, Karaköy
Tel: 0212 292 3992 www.safranist.com
Open: 7pm–4am. Closed Sundays and June–Sept.

The 200-year-old building that Safran occupies is attractive inside and out. The modern interior decorative motif of rapidly alternating brightly coloured lights doesn't detract too much from

the beautifully patterned tiling, simple on the floor and more elaborate on the walls. Whether the affluent, professional crowd who populate Safran are paying much attention to them is doubtful; they're too busy downing the relatively expensive cocktails and dancing to the pop and house tunes spun by DJ and owner Asli Altan, one of a number of bar/club owning ex-actresses in Istanbul. Typically for a city whose inhabitants consider a night on the tiles without indigestion as being a night not worth experiencing, Safran doubles as a restaurant serving good Mediterranean and Turkish dishes.

Sapphire Bosphorus, Muallim Naci Caddesi 27, Kuruçeşme
Tel: 0532 371 2200
Open: 6pm–4am daily

Reina has a massive picture of a Porsche decorating its entrance. Sapphire Bosphorus has a display including an actual SUV from, er, Toyota. What seems like a terrible fashion faux pas in the world of conspicuous consumption to the obviously uninitiated is ignored by the glam Kuruçeşme set who flock here in droves, Toyota or no Toyota. Indistinguishable (because they're the same people) from the clientele at Angelique, Sortie, Reina et al, they come here to appreciate the Bosphorus from a slightly different

visual angle and enjoy the slightly different décor. With an emphasis on slightly. The outside terrace is nice – though it's not right on the waterfront – with dark wood decking and comfy sofas interspersed among the more formal tables.

Sortie, Muallim Naci Caddesi 141/142, Kuruçeşme
Tel: 0212 327 8585
Open: 6pm–5am daily

Until last year Sortie was Leila, Turkish celebrity central and the most famous club alongside Reina on the Kuruçeşme strip. Now it's called Sortie and is Turkish celebrity central, only slightly less

famous (for the moment). The same crowd as before frequent the place, happily dropping several hundred dollars a night each on the overpriced food, champagne and cocktails. But you're paying for the company. Not their conversation, of course, which, even if it were worth listening to, is drowned out by the loud pop-pap broadcast by the DJs, but their aesthetic and social presence. Like its rivals Sortie is certainly blessed in attractive customers and so worth a visit, along with all its rivals (just to make sure). Bring your Amex Black, or just spray paint your debit card.

Zarifi, Çukurluçeşme Sokak 13, Çukurcuma
Tel: 0212 293 5480
Open: midday–2am. Closed Sundays and May–mid-Sept.

Okay it's more of a restaurant than a club, but you should only book into Zarifi (rammed on prime nights, so booking is essential) if you're interested in a raucous night out involving a good bit of dancing and loud music, which is basically clubbing. The food, Turkish, Greek and Arabic, is perfectly good; though it's not a headliner on the bill, it does come first. The very elegantly decorated interior fills up with a smart crowd, generally in their late 20s to 40s, around 9–10pm with people typically dining in large groups. As the evening progresses and the *meze* are washed down with increasing amounts of *rakı* and wine, the in-house DJs beginning cranking up the volume on the Turkish and oriental

pop hits and the fun starts. First, it's just a few more exuberant
types waving their arms around to the music, then a few stand
up, others get on chairs, and soon the table-tops are as crowded
as the dance-floor. The peak comes when the live entertainment

takes over from the DJs, especially when it's a band of attractive
Roma drummers who beat out atavistic rhythms and send the
place crazy. The restaurant refuses to release statistics on how
many customers die of heart attacks but it must be a significant
number. A good, totally unpretentious Turkish night out.

MUSIC CLUBS

Mojo, Büyükparmakkapı Sokak 26, Beyoğlu
Tel: 0212 243 2927 www.mojomusic.org
Open: 10pm–4am daily

'I'm going down to Louisiana/ gonna get me a mojo hand/ gonna
have all you girls under my command' - that's what Muddy
Waters said anyway. It's a good distance from Louisiana and one
hopes (probably in vain) its clientele have rather more refined
attitudes to their opposite genders, but in its dark, basement
space Mojo serves up rock'n'roll and blues acts and lots of beer.

Nardis Jazz Club, Galata Kulesi Sokak 14, Galata
Tel: 0212 244 6327 www.nardisjazz.com
Open: 7pm–1.30am Mon–Sat

At the top of one of the roads that slopes away from Galata
Tower is the city's top jazz venue, Nardis Jazz Club, run by gui-
tarist Onder Focan. The simple contemporary fittings in the old
building work well, but that's beside the point. This is a small but
serious jazz club and not a place for chatting or admiring the
décor. The music starts from 9.30pm onwards and is top-notch.
You can eat and drink (quietly) and book ahead if you want a
table near the stage.

Roxy, Aslan Yatağı Sokak 3, Beyoğlu
Tel: 0212 245 6539
Open: 9pm–3am (5am Fri/Sat) Wed–Sat. Closed July–Sept.

In a side street off Sıraselviler Caddesi, Roxy is one Istanbul's best known music and club venues, hosting bands, DJs and electronica outfits as well as more unusual theatrical performances. It's also a regular dance club playing an eclectic mix of funk, soul, disco, etc. that attracts a young, faithful following. It's also open to 5am at weekends if you're looking for a late night drink.

culture...

It has been Istanbul's fate, over centuries, to be at the epicentre of enormous shifts in geopolitical power from East to West and back again. The city was originally Hellenic, became subsumed and shaped by the Romans, who in their turn were moulded by indigenous traditions and those of the East in general, before finally being supplanted by the Ottomans. After centuries of vitality the late Ottomans crumbled before the ever-increasing power of Western Europe. In the last major plot twist, coming after the empire's disastrous defeat in World War I, Mustafa Kemal Atatürk, a gifted general, packed the last Sultan onto the Orient Express with a one-way outward-bound ticket, and created the modern, Westernized, nationalistic republic that Turkey is today.

The city still bears the mark of each culture that has lived within it, so that to walk through its older areas is to explore an open archaeological site in which the layers of history are visible to all.

Aside from the awesome Hagia Sophia, much of old Byzantium lies hidden. The great Byzantine palace that once covered much of Sultanahmet is the city's great lost monument, but its substructures are still there, accessible through the odd cellar. Of the once great Hippodrome, only the area of its spine, replete with obelisks, is still visible. At the Church of Christ in Chora, however, until recently relatively neglected by visitors, a stunning mosaic interior is on view.

The Ottomans took up the grand building tradition of the Romans with gusto, but it took them a century to match the challenge of the Hagia Sophia's dome and ethereal interior. Mimar Sinan, the great Ottoman architect, equal to any produced by Renaissance Europe, built the Süleymaniye Mosque for

Süleyman the Magnificent. Sited on the city's highest hill it is imposing, but as with the Hagia Sophia, it is the soaring lightness of its interior, an attempt to create a heavenly space on earth, wherein lies the genius of its architecture. Of the late Ottomans, the Bosphorus palaces, starting with the Dolmabahçe, are indicative, with their attempt to meld Eastern and Western traditions some-times elegant, often messy, while several Art Nouveau architectural gems are reminders that early 20th-century Istanbul was as fashionable as any city in Europe.

It is a source of irritation to those involved in Turkish contemporary life that in Istanbul culture is generally regarded as an historical concept, but there are few modern cultural attractions that justify tearing oneself away from the old. The Atatürk Cultural Centre occasionally stages concerts of Ottoman classical music, while in earthier venues off İstiklal Caddesi you can hear Turkish folk music and its cousin, Fasıl, which combines strains of classical, gypsy and folk in one. The recent opening of Istanbul Modern, meanwhile, rounds off a decade of growth in the status and visibility of Turkish contemporary art.

Advanced ironists will want to indulge in more touristy manifestations of local 'culture' and will enjoy the its-so-bad-its-wonderful 'Belly dancing and Harem Show' atop the Galata Tower. They may also wish to join the intensely indolent at MiniaTürk – not a cabaret act by Turkish midgets, but a theme-park of maquettes of Turkey's top attractions, where you can study the great mosques and marvel at the ancient city of Ephesus, all at 1/25th of their actual size and within easy walking distance of each other.

Approach to the city by water

Until the Orient Express pulled into Sinkeci Station in 1883 at the end of its maiden journey, most Westerners first saw Istanbul from

the water. Today's taxi ride from Atatürk International Airport is more efficient but rather less spectacular. It is only by re-creating that approach to the city by water, which, at its simplest you can do by getting the ferry back to the Old City from the Asian shore, that you get a true hint of the psychological impact felt by genera-tions of visitors on their first vision of the city. From the water the massiveness of the Hagia Sophia, and the great Blue Mosque and Süleymaniye are all the more powerful and surreal, the city more exotic. Their effect on one, admittedly famously romantic, eye is recorded in Byron's epic poem *Don Juan*: 'The European with the Asian shore/ Sprinkled with palaces; the Ocean stream/ Here and there studded with a seventy-four;/ Sophia's cupola with golden gleam;/ The cypress groves; Olympus high and hoar;/ The twelve isles, and the more than I could dream…'

**Archaeology Museum (Arkeolojii Müzesi),
Osman Hamdi Bey Yokuğu, Gülhane**
Tel: 0212 520 7740
Open: 9am–5pm. Closed Mondays.

It's unsurprising that a city with such a history should have such a superb archaeological museum, nevertheless its collection (of which only a fraction is on show) is superb. You could spend several days within its 20 galleries. But here are some highlights. The museum was founded in order to house its most famous artefact, the Alexander Sarcophagus. Part of the necropolis of the Phrygian Kings found in a Lebanese field just over a century ago, it is a 4th-century marble sarcophagus, its sides bearing exquisitely carved bas-reliefs depicting Alexander the Great's wars with the Persians. Much to the chagrin of its discoverers, though, it's not actually Alexander's tomb. After inspecting that and the wonderful classical statuary have a look at Istanbul through the Ages, a permanent exhibition that tells the story of the city through several evocative pieces, including a section of the great chain that the Byzantines used to pull across the Bosphorous to block invading ships. To end on a positive note have a look at the world's earliest peace treaty, the treaty of Kadesh agreed in 1269 BC between the Hittites and the Egyptian pharaoh Ramses II and carved into tablets on show in the next door building, the Museum of the Ancient Orient.

Atatürk Museum, Halaskargazi Caddesi 250, Şişli
Tel: 0212 233 4723
Open: 9am–4pm. Closed Sundays and Mondays.

It's impossible to understand modern Turkey without understanding the remarkable Mustafa Kemal Atatürk. As a brilliant young general he soundly defeated the Allies at Gallipoli and then rose up against the Greeks who occupied parts of Turkey after its defeat in World War I and kicked them out. The last sultan soon followed them, with a one-way outward-bound train ticket on the Orient Express. In 1923 Turkey became a secular republic and Mustafa Kemal adopted the name Atatürk 'Father of

the Turks' and the presidency. Still more remarkable than this is that in seeking to reverse the decline of the late Ottoman period and in his attempt to build a modern secular industrial state, Atatürk re-forged an entire culture. He changed the language, exorcising foreign words, changed habits and costumes, and banned the word Constantinople and the seemingly innocuous *fes* among other things, and in doing so practically re-invented the Turkish identity. Atatürk's honorific title was well deserved. He died in 1938 but Turkey is still enamoured with his image and memory. The museum is a short taxi ride away from Taksim Square and houses three floors of Atatürk memorabilia including, wonderfully, his underpants. While not the world's best museum it's a good place to go to and think – and get to grips the legacy of the man.

The Bosphorus Tour

The first words go to the 18th-century satirist and poet Lady

Montagu: 'The pleasure of going on a barge to Chelsea is not
comparable to that of rowing upon the canal of the sea here,
where, for twenty miles together down the Bosphorus, the most
beautiful variety of prospects present themselves.' Indeed. Back
then the green and tree-lined shores of the Bosphorus, which
stretches 14 miles from the Sea of Marmara to the Black Sea,
were studded with villages and *yalıs*, the beautiful, wooden, sometimes fabulously ornate, summer houses wealthy Ottomans built
for themselves. Studies in the art of aligning human pleasure
within the frame of nature, they are among the most refined and
civilized houses humans have ever built, hedonistic even, in the
true sense of the word. Today the Bosphorus shores are still
among the world's prime stretches of real estate, and more's the
pity for urban sprawl and developers mean that Mary Montagu
had far more charming views than we do. However, on a beautiful day the Bosphorus is still magical and there are plenty of

wonderful sights along the way – the beautiful 19th-century
Büyük Mecidiye Mosque by the first, massive suspension bridge
in Oratköy, the twin fortresses of Rumeli and Andalou by the
second bridge, the decaying beauty of the Köprülü Yalı in
Amcazade, the kitschly baroque Muhayyeş Yalı in Yeniköy, Sultan
Abdülaziz's summer palace in Beylerbeyi, and more. You can
either take the ferry all the way up the Bosphorus and back,
which will take six hours, or a shorter ferry journey as far as the
Rumeli Hisarı, or even take a private boat for a tour (see Info
section for details).

Calligraphy Museum, Beyazit Square, Beyazit
Tel: 0212 527 5851
Open: 9am–4pm. Closed Sundays and Mondays.

Famously Islam forbids the depiction of living beings in art. This
isn't strictly true (the depiction of the living creatures in a non-

sacred context is allowed in some Muslim cultures) but certainly
Muslim and Ottoman artists spent their time not trying to mimic
nature as Westerners did but, instead, creating more abstract
beauty in the calligraphy and patterned decoration, notably in the
famous *tuğras*, or calligraphic emblems-cum-signatures of the
sultans. Although the Museum's collection has literally fragment-
ed as a result of disgraceful incompetence over the years, there
are several beautiful things to see here, especially the illuminated
Korans, and it is worth a detour from the nearby Grand Bazaar.

**Church of Christ in the Chora (Kariye Camii),
Kariye Camii Sohak 26, Edirnekapi**
Tel: 0212 631 9241
Open: 9am–4.30pm. Closed Wednesdays.

Truly jewel-like, the modestly sized Church of Christ in the
Chora is a visual delight, adorned with some of finest remaining
examples of Byzantine art in the world. The church's name is
explained by a mosaic above the entrance depicting the Virgin

Mary shown with Christ in the womb. Inscribed are the words 'container [*chora*] of the uncontainable'. The theme of the containers is taken up with gusto in mosaic scenes of miracles such as the turning of water into wine and the Feeding of the Five Thousand in which jugs of wine and baskets of bread take pride of place, all of which cast tupperware in a new light. There is a mosaic depicting the Enrolment for Taxation, which one historian describes as possibly 'the greatest glorification of tax collection in the history of art'. The 14th-century art inadvertently owes its preservation to the Muslims who converted the place to a mosque, covering and thus protecting the frescos and mosaics with plaster. Now it's a museum. Next door to the church is the Kariye Hotel, with its Ottoman restaurant Asitane, which you might like to try. Nearby are the city walls.

City Walls

Stretching from the Sea of Marmara to the Golden Horn, the great walls built by Emperor Theodosius II in the 5th century formed the western boundary of the Old City for a thousand years till they were breached with some finality by the Ottomans in 1453. Today the ruins still give one a sense of their once near mythical indomitability. You can walk the length of the wall, sometimes on top of it. You could start at either one of the ends, at the Yedikule Fortress by the Sea of Marmara or the ruined Byzantine Blachernae palace on the Golden Horn. Notable

points along the way include the Gate of Romanos, where
Constantine XI, the last emperor, fell before Mehmet's army, and
Edirnekapı, where Mehmet made his victorious entry. Sadly,

though opinions will differ on this, sections of the wall are being
'rebuilt' in a misguided attempt to recreate their former glory.

Dolmabahçe Palace, Dolmabahçe Caddesi, Beşiktas
Tel: 0212 236 9000
Open: 9am–4pm. Closed Mondays, Thursdays and Saturdays.

The clearest proof of the Europeanization of the Ottoman court
came when Sultan Abdülmecit (1839–62) abandoned his ances-
tral home of the Topkapı, finding it a little too medieval for his

sophisticated Francophile tastes, and built the massive, baroque Italianate palace on the Bosphorus, nearer the modern action of Beyoğlu. It took 11 years to build and was finished just before the outbreak of the Crimean War, in time for Abdülmecit to receive the European emissaries of his allies in its vast throne room. The superbly self-important ornate, baroque and rococo style speaks of a building designed to impress through sheer visual attrition, hoping that the onlooker's quality control mechanism will cease to function in the face of all those embellishments. Significantly for the palace's status in the national psyche, Atatürk died in a big walnut bed in a room on the second floor in 1938.

**Galata Mevelevihanesi (Whirling Dervishes),
Galip Dede Caddesi 15, Tünel**
Tel: 0212 245 4141
Open: 9.30am–4.30pm. Closed Tuesdays.
Show: 5pm Sundays, May–Sept.

Whirling Dervishes! Along with everything else that smacked of the bad retrograde Ottoman days, the Whirling Dervishes were banned in the brave new world of the Turkish republic.

Eventually, however, the government took pity on the hordes of visiting tourists and allowed the Galata Mevelevihanesi to stage shows. It's the only official Dervish lodge in town. Founded by the Persian mystic Rumi in the 13th century in Konya, eastern Turkey, the Dervishes are essentially an archaic bunch of hippies who, according to their literature, believe 'the fundamental condition of our existence is to revolve' and aim their revolutions towards attaining true love and so on. The building is also known as the Museum for Classical Literature, housing a number of beautiful musical instruments and illuminated Korans. The Dervish shows on summer Sundays are always packed with camcording tourists but unless you want to spend time in the murky world of underground Dervishes it's all you're gonna get (actually it's still quite spectacular).

Galata Tower, Galata Square, Beyoğlu
Tel: 0212 293 8180
Open: 9am–8pm daily

Built in 1348 by the Genoese who lived in its shadow (after it was built, obviously), the heavy and distinctively fat cylindrical form of Galata Tower was converted by the Ottomans into a

prison for captives taken in battle. Nowadays the leg-irons are gone but its Turkish management (possibly direct descendants of the original jailors) still inflicts punishment on foreigners in the form of theatrical 'touristic' entertainment, including the Harem Show and belly-dancing. However, if you go during the day you can avoid their clutches and instead enjoy the fabulous 360°

views, some of the best in the city.

Greek Orthodox Patriarchate,
Sadrazam Ali Paşa Caddesi, Fener
Open: 9am–5pm daily

The global centre of the Greek Orthodox faith for three centuries, the Patriarchate, built in 1720, is found in an initially unattractive walled compound in the western district of the Old City

called Fener. Its lavish interior, especially its golden altar screen, is eye-catching though not particularly outstanding as these things go. But if you catch a service here you'll get a distinct sense of the culture and ceremonial tradition of the Greek Orthodox Church and so catch a glimpse of the religion that dominated Constantinople for a millennium.

Hagia Sophia, Ayasofya Müzesi, Sultanahmet
Tel: 0212 528 4500
Open: 9am–7pm. Closed Mondays.

If you can only see one building in Istanbul, see the Hagia Sophia. For a thousand years this was the largest building on earth, but its power was not due to gross size alone. The Byzantine historian Procopius saw it being built. To him the Hagia Sophia's vast dome was a miracle: 'A spherical-shaped domed standing upon

this circle is exceedingly beautiful; from the lightness of the building, it does not appear to rest on a solid foundation, but to
cover the place beneath as though it were suspended from heav-

en by the fabled golden chain.' Built by the great Byzantine
emperor Justinian (it was finished in AD 537), it's hard to overes-
timate its importance over the subsequent centuries in the imag-
inations of both friends and foes of Constantinople, generating
the kind of awe in contemporaries that New York's skyline
would in those who have never seen a city before. But not
because of its exterior, which is unlovely and heavy on the eye.
The magic, as Procopious understood, was inside. The idea of the
interior was to be a place of awe that in its spaciousness, the
improbability of its dome, the gleam of its gold mosaics in the
candlelight, the scent of incense, transported, almost literally, the
worshipper to a heavenly place. Such responses belong to another time, but the architecture and the mosaics are still otherworldly.

Hippodrome, At Meydanı, Sultanahmet

All that is left of Constantinople's once mighty Hippodrome,
which by the 4th century could seat 100,000 spectators, is the
long, rectangular area of At Meydanı (Horse Square) in front of
the Sultanahmet Mosque. It was the *spina*, or central reservation,
around which the charioteers would race with reckless ferocity,
much to everyone's amusement. The vertical relics that survive

are among the most ancient artefacts in the city, including the 5th-century BC Serpentine Column, nicked from the Temple of Apollo at Delphi, and the Egyptian obelisk, carved around 1,500 BC and filched from Karnak. The emperor Theodosius had it set on a marble pedestal carved with scenes celebrating his enjoyment of the races. It takes a considerable mental leap to recreate the noise and excitement inspired by the Romans' favourite

pastime. Indeed only the most imaginatively violent football hooligan could come close to comprehending the intense rivalry between the two chariot-racing factions, the Blues and the Greens, which dominated Byzantine life. The Niké Riots, which briefly threatened the throne of Justinian, ended in the massacre of 35,000 of the Green faction by the triumphant Blues, which puts even the rivalry between Istanbul's football teams into perspective.

Kız Kulesi, The Maiden's Tower, Üsküdar

One of Istanbul's most famous landmarks is, strangely, the Kız Kulesi, the Maiden's Tower, but better known in the English-speaking world as Leander's Tower. The latter name refers to the old Greek legend of Leander who died swimming to see his beautiful lover Hero. But that was supposed to have happened at the Dardanelles, on the other side of the Sea of Marmara. The myth of the maiden in the tower is archetypal, attached to many buildings in the region, about a girl being locked in a tower to confound a prophecy that she'd die of a snake-bite. But sadly the snake arrives in a bowl of fruit and she cops it anyway. In any case the building, just offshore of Üsküdar, is actually a small,

squat tower, built in the last century, which has done nothing more heroic than serve as a lighthouse. But it's a nice place to sip tea and contemplate the Bosphorus.

 ### Milion, near Divan Yolu, Sultanahmet

At the crossroads opposite the Hagia Sophia, walking towards Diyvn Yolu, there is a unassuming broken stone column rising up from a bricked recess. It is the Milion or milestone, once probably tiled in gold. In AD 324 Constantine made it the point from which all distances in the Roman Empire would be measured. It

was for a while the symbolic centre of much of the world.

MiniaTürk, İmrahor Caddesi, Sütlücem
Tel: 0212 222 2882 www.miniaturk.com.tr
Open: 10am–7pm Mon–Fri; 10am–9pm Sat–Sun

Bored with worthy monuments? Pushed for time? Then
MiniaTürk, located on the Golden Horn, could be the ticket for
you, being a large park with 105 splendid models of the historical
and cultural sites of Turkey all at 1:25 scale. See the Aspendos
Theatre, the Süleymaniye Mosque, the Sumela Monastery, as well

as a mini Bosphorus with ships sailing beneath. There is also a
miniature railway network, a motorway with moving vehicles and
an airport with thousands of human figures and moving planes. If
you're a child, or can pass yourself off as one, you can also enjoy
the MiniaTürk Express, an electric mini train giving up to 24 little
people a fun-packed ride through the park.

**Mosaic Museum, Büyüksaray Mozaik, Arasta Bazaar,
Sultanahmet**
Tel: 0212 518 1205
Open: 9am–4.30pm. Closed Sundays.

Hidden away behind one end of the Arasta Bazaar, next to the
Sultanahmet Mosque, is an unprepossessing building that houses
a mosaic floor, part of the great Byzantine palace that once

covered the area, a fragment of the city's great 'missing monument'. The mosaic depicts bucolic and mythological scenes as
well as charming vignettes showing animals ripping each other

apart, revealing the Byzantine's sophisticated sadistic side. It's well
worth a quick visit to get a hint of what the area looked like a
millennia-and-a-half ago.

Rumeli Hisari, Yahya Kemal Caddesi, Rumeli Hisari
Open: 9am–4.30pm. Closed Sundays.

The appearance of the massive form of Rumeli Hisari (*Hisari*
meaning castle) on the European shore of the Bosphorus in the
summer of 1452 signalled the doom of Byzantium. Built in only
four months to face Anadolu Hisari across the narrowest point

of the Bosphorus, it was part of Mehmet the Conquerer's plan to isolate the city by destroying any ship attempting to ferry supplies to the city. Thus it was nicknamed Boğazkesen (the throat cutter) and immediately on completion sunk a foolhardy Venetian merchant ship with its long-range cannon. Now it plays host to more pacific activities, such as open-air theatrical and musical events through the summer nights.

St Stephen's Cathedral, Mürsel Paşa Caddesi 85-7, Fener
Tel: 0212 521 1121
Open: no formal visiting hours

The cathedral of St Stephen of the Bulgars on the shore of the Golden Horn is notable on two counts. It is one of the few examples of neo-Gothic architecture, but more impressive is the fact that it's a pre-fab, constructed entirely out of cast-iron sections, cast in Vienna and brought to Istanbul down the Danube on a hundred barges. It was built, or rather bolted together, in 1871 for the Bulgarian community who were allowed by the

Ottomans to split from the Greek Orthodox faith and found their own Bulgarian Church. Despite being neo-Gothic and made of iron it's a pretty church still used by the dwindling local Bulgarian community and best visited on Sunday mornings as there are no formal visiting times.

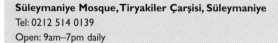
The crowning achievement of Ottoman architectural-superstar Mimar Sinan and symbolic of the glory of the reign of Süleyman the Magnificent, the Süleymaniye is the Ottoman riposte to the Hagia Sophia. Unlike the Byzantine builders, Sinan was interested in making an impact externally, locating the mosque on the Old City's highest hill and designing a series of smaller domes cascading off the central structure and supporting its weight. But like the Hagia Sophia, whose plan it follows, it is the interior that really matters. Its sense of the space and the elegant lightness with which the vast span and size of the dome is supported are

an amazing architectural and engineering feat, an expression of power and technological sophistication at once subtle and awesome. More than any other individual in history Sinan has left his physical mark on the city as author of a vast number of buildings (477 throughout Turkey), obviously operating a workshop-cum-architectural practice of some size. Born of Christian parents in 1490 he was taken into imperial service as a child, working as a military engineer before becoming Chief Architect to Süleyman the Magnificent in 1538.

Sultanahmet (Blue) Mosque, Meydad Sokak, Sultanahmet
Tel: 0212 518 1319
Open: 9am–9pm (7pm Nov–Apr) daily. Sound and light show May–Oct after dusk daily.

Built by Mehmet Ağa, a pupil of Sinan's, for Sultan Ahmet I and finished in 1616 it became popularly known as the Blue Mosque, owing to the profusion of blue Iznik tiles that cover much of its interior. The six minarets with which Mehmet Ağa furnished the mosque were a cause of controversy, as the Grand Mecca at

Mecca, the holiest site in Islam, also had six. Perhaps he was trying to draw attention away from the interior, which lacks the elegance, gracefulness and engineering genius of either the Hagia Sophia or the Süleymaniye. The dome here is far more obviously supported by the thick pillars, thus spoiling the conceit of a sacred, inhumanly wrought architecture. It is still pretty impressive from the outside, though.

Topkapı Palace Museum, Sultanahmet, Eminönü
Tel: 0212 512 0408
Open: 9am–4pm. Closed Tuesdays.

Built by Mehmet the Conqueror the Topkapı was the palace of sultans for some 400 years and the epicentre of the mystique and baroque majesty of the Ottoman dynasty. Sited on a promontory overlooking the confluence of the Golden Horn and the Bosphorus, the Topkapı was actually the second palace Mehmet built, having erected one by the Golden Horn as soon

as he got his hands on the city. Some have speculated that a little sightseeing (combined with war) of Mehmet's own in Athens inspired him to live where the Byzantine's acropolis once stood. For whatever reason, he started again. The Topkapı owes its form more to a military encampment than to the grand sacred or monumental architecture of the Greeks or Romans, being a collection of reasonably proportioned buildings built around a succession of courtyards and thus preserving a memory of the Turks' past as nomadic warriors. The fantastically ornate decorative styling that adorns so many of the buildings is, however, a far cry from your average tent decoration. The place is large and often packed with visitors, so to maximize your viewing pleasure try going as early as possible. If you have limited time, have a quick stroll around the complex and then dive into the famous Treasury and the Harem (you need additional tickets for both areas). The Treasury is filled with the most exquisitely ornamented artefacts from centuries of collecting and creating imperial opulence. The Harem, meanwhile, a complex of 300 intensely decorated rooms, can only be seen as part of a half-hour-long official tour.

**Turkish and Islamic Art Museum, At Meydam 46,
Sultanahmet**
Tel: 0212 518 1805
Open: 9am–5pm. Closed Mondays.

The gloriousness of the Museum's building didn't do any favours for its first owner, Ibrahim Paşa, Grand Vezir to Süleyman I. The Sultan was convinced by his scheming wife Roxelana to get rid of (i.e. strangle) Ibrahim whose vaunting ambition, she felt, was symbolized by the grandeur of his home. Now the old palace,

which overlooks the Hippodrome, houses a collection of assorted examples of Islamic arts: manuscripts, carpets, miniatures, woodwork, metalwork and glasswork, which originated from all corners of the Ottoman empire. Especially notable are old, large, Seljuk and Ottoman mosque carpets.

**Underground Cistern (Yerebatan Cistern),
Yerebatan Caddesi, Sultanahmet**
Tel: 0212 522 1259
Open: 9am–4pm. Closed Mondays.

The Underground Cistern is another tourist attraction, like the Maiden's Tower, which is completely undeserving of its status, being pretty insignificant on every level, but which you should know about it because it'll get mentioned somewhere else and you might get curious and waste more time trying to find out about it (or going to it) than you are by reading this. It was discovered in the 16th century by visiting Frenchman Petrus Gyllius, who

had little time for the 'Carelessness and Contempt of everything that is curious in the inhabitants [of Istanbul]' and went poking around in cellars. He found this 6th-century part of the Byzantine's complex, an impressive cistern system that houses the city's reservoirs of water. Now it's full of coloured light and New-Agey sounds.

ART

İstanbul Modern, Meclis-I Mebusan Caddesi, Liman İşletmeleri Sahası, Antrepo 4, Karaköy
Tel: 0212 334 7300 www.istanbulmodern.org
Open: 10am–6pm (8pm Thurs). Closed Mondays.

Visual art has been the most internationally successful of Turkey's contemporary art forms, along with the novels of Orhan Pamuk. Such artists as Kutlug Ataman, Haluk Acache and the fashion-designer-turned-artist Hussein Challayan are big names on the global gallery circuit, while the domestic scene has taken root. The opening of Istanbul Modern in late 2004, built by the philanthropic Eczacıbaşı family, the country's foremost cultural patrons (far ahead of the government), set a symbolic seal on all that success. For the moment, however, it's full of 19th- and 20th-century European-style Turkish art, which isn't the best. A contemporary programme is getting going, however, and the museum is worth a visit to see a more modern side of Turkish culture. The café and restaurant are also very good.

Other easily accessible places to see contemporary art in Istanbul are Platform, a non-profit gallery sponsored by Garanti Bank on İstiklal Caddesi, run by Istanbul Biennale curator Varsif Kortun and British curator November Paynter (www.platform.garanti.com.tr); and Galerist, the city's top commercial gallery, also on İstiklal Caddesi (www.galerist.com.tr).

CLASSICAL AND OTTOMAN CLASSICAL MUSIC

 Atatürk Cultural Centre, Taksim Square, Taksim
Tel: 0212 251 5600

On Taksim Square, the brutalist 1970s form of the Atatürk Cultural Centre is the city's premier performing arts venue and the place to go if you want to catch some classical – or more interestingly Ottoman – classical music while you're in town. The State Opera and Ballet, the Symphony Orchestra and the State Theatre Company all share the same venue.

Kallavi 20, Kallavi Sokak 20, off İstiklal Caddesi, Galatasaray, Beyoğlu
Tel: 0212 251 1010
Open: midday–3pm, 7pm–1am. Closed Sundays.

Why simply have a cultural experience when you can have a gastronomic, cultural and entertainment experience all in one? After a trip to one of the many bars (*meyhanes*) that play Turkish folk

or its related musical cousin *fasıl*, which combines strains of classical, gypsy and folk, it's not hard to see why Western-style pop hasn't come to dominate Turkey's music culture completely. Kallavi 20, a *meyhane*, just off İstiklal Caddesi, as are many similar venues, is one of the best places to go to hear *fasıl*. As your meal progresses and increasing amounts of *rakı* are consumed, the *fasıl* band, who are usually Roma playing drum, violin, clarinet and zither, trots out and skilfully starts building up the tempo till the little reserve that the Turks possess is completely swept away, along with the tables, in an orgy of handclapping and jigging about. Reservations recommended.

İal, Büyükparmakkapi Sokak 14, off İstiklal Caddesi, Beyoğlu
Tel: 0212 243 4196

Just over the road from the veggie Nature & Peace restaurant, (see Snack) on the easy to annunciate Büyükparmakkapi Sokak off İstiklal, is İal, where you might like to sample Turkish folk, along with a beer or two. The intimate, low-ceilinged room gets even more intimate when the music hits its stride, with the traditional pipe playing inspiring some raucous dancing. Typically for such places, İal also serves up some good, simple Turkish dishes.

BELLY DANCING

Then there's belly dancing. Just as the word 'actress' was once considered a euphemism for prostitute in polite Western society, so were belly dancers considered women of ill repute by respectable Turks. Since the 1970s, however, belly dancing has become widely acceptable and even appreciated. The comely Sertap Erener triumphed in the 2003 Eurovision song contest, not least thanks to her belly-flinging skills.

Galata Tower, Galata Square, Beyoğlu
Tel: 0212 293 8180
Show: 8pm daily

A touristic extravaganza of belly dancing and other joys, at the top of Galata Tower, for a mere 65 YTL a head.

Kazablanka, Kuytu Sokak 4, off Tarlabaşhı Bulvarı, Beyoğlu
Tel: 0212 247 1630
Show: 9pm–midnight daily

shop...

Shopping is in the lifeblood of Istanbul. The city owed much of its past fame and fortune to its perfect location at the centre of ancient trade routes between East and West and even now the Bosphorus presents the spectacle of a constant parade of container ships ferrying everything from agricultural produce to narcotics, to and from the Black Sea ports and the world at large.

The city has always consumed its fair share of that trade and all the exchange had to be housed somewhere. So with considerable foresight Mehmet the Conqueror founded the Kapalı Carşhi – the Grand Bazaar – in 1461. It is now the oldest shopping mall in the world, a city unto itself of around 5,500 shops, attracting tourists and locals alike with the rarefied allure of fine carpets, precious antiques and artfully wrought jewellery as well as the quotidian promise of acres of fake label handbags and dirt-cheap clothes. Finding one's way through, or even surviving, the bewildering array of stores and products, the noise, the hawkers and the essential haggling requires a tough sensibility, but a visit to what is the greatest oriental bazaar of them all is rightly considered de rigueur.

Other bazaars in the old city deserve attention. The Arasta Bazaar, originally built to help finance the Sultanahmet mosque in whose shadow it lies, is a small but high-quality and genteel alternative to the Kapalı Carşhi (salesmen are banned from harassing the passersby), housing some of the city's most

reputable dealers in carpets, rare Turkish and Asian textiles and ceramics. Among more touristy wares on sale at the Egyptian Spice Bazaar, near Galata Bridge, are superb spices, honey, nuts, coffee and other earthy products. The relative cheapness of the caviar, both Iranian and Russian (from the Caspian), deserves special mention and perhaps the preparatory packing of cool bags.

Over the bridge Beyoğlu offers more contemporary attractions. Towards the top of the steep hill that climbs from Galata Tower into town is a cluster of music shops, including those selling specialized Turkish instruments. Nearby quality antiques and high-class (some quite pricey) retro items, reminders of Istanbul's cosmopolitan 19th-century past, fill the charming shops and boutiques of Çukurcuma, a once dilapidated area recently gentrified into an Istanbulli equivalent of Portobello. Meanwhile the huge, pedestrianized, thoroughfare that is İstiklal Caddesi promises everything one could want (and much more one does not want) from a modern high-street shopping experience. Be sure not to miss Hacı Bekir, the eponymous store founded in 1777 by the inventor of *lokum* (Turkish delight), amid the confusion of shop fronts.

Fashionistas and label addicts will have to head still further north where the chic district of Nişantaşı is home to sleek, international and home-grown designer boutiques as well as upmarket department stores such as Beyman. The highlights here are those who creatively update their Turkish and Ottoman heritage, including designer Gönül Paksoy, whose contemporary-fashioned Ottoman fabrics would look equally good framed as worn, and her sister Sema Paksoy, who incorporates exquisite historical fragments into her contemporary jewellery works.

Built to finance the Sultanhamet Mosque's charitable projects, the Arasta Bazaar is a single row of shops running alongside the mosque's eastern wall. It houses some of the most respected merchants in Istanbul and also has the delightful advantage of having banned touting among its tenants. If you're pressed for time and can't do the Grand Bazaar properly (or can't face it) then this is a good, quick alternative.

Galeri Gengiz – run by business partners, both called Gengiz, who are among the most respected carpet dealers in the city
Iznik Classics – high-quality reproductions of antique Iznik ceramics
Maison du Tapis d'Orient – a superb, expertly sourced selection of Central Asian fabrics and clothes
Otağ – fascinating range of unusual Central Asian musical instruments; intriguing for serious musicians (who like Central Asia)

Also known as the Spice Bazaar, the Egyptian Bazaar is an L-shaped hall located by the New Mosque, near Galata Bridge in Eminönü. It's always packed with tourists (blame yourself – I do) and superficially full of the rubbish that tourist love to buy.

However, there are some excellent food shops and delis, which should not be missed. If you get hungry looking at all that food you can head upstairs to the famous, still smart and attractive Pandeli restaurant. Alternatively find and study the wares of one of the leech sellers to be found among the pet merchants. That might put you off eating for a while.

Cankurtaran – exquisite honey from all over Turkey
Doğu Pazarı – for your consignment of cheap but good Azerbaijani caviar
Erzincanlilar – superb deli for honeycomb and hard Turkish cheese
Kurukahveci Mehmet Efendi – 1930s shop selling the best Turkish coffee money can buy
Malata Pazarı – for dried fruit and nuts
Papağan – nuts, mulberries, figs and other delights

Grand Bazaar

The spiritual home of shopping in Istanbul, the Grand Bazaar is an extraordinary city unto itself, divided into mini-suburbs of one specialization or another. At its heart is the İc Bedesten (Inner Bazaar), the ancient and comparatively genteel home of many of the market's most respected merchants, dealing in the highest value items, antiques, metalwork and curios. To its north and west are the carpet dealers, to its south and east, jewellers and gold and silver merchants. In the bazaars far west are the fabric and leather dealers. Shopping here seriously takes at least half a day, allowing time for looking, comparing, getting tired, looking again, haggling, arguing, and possibly storming off and starting the whole process somewhere else. But that would be bad manners, as you shouldn't enter into protracted bargaining unless you intend to buy. For that vital rest, bite to eat and stimulating coffee look for the Fez Café (Halıcılar Caddesi just north of the İc Bedesten), Julia's Kitchen (Keseciler Caddesi, south of the İc Bedesten) or Sark Kahvesi (corner of Yağlıkçıar Caddesi and Fesciler Caddesi).

With 5,500 shops (including 1,600 jewellers alone), on 65 streets, the selection below amounts only to a few highlights.

Abdullah L. Chalabi, Sandal Bedesten Sokak 6 – trading since 1880 in top-quality European and Ottoman antique jewellery
Abdulla Natural Products, Halıcılar Caddesi 53 – 100% natural, handmade textiles and soaps
Adıyaman Pazarı, Yağlıkçıar Caddesi 74–46 – top dealer in Gaziantep weaves, the highly coloured, traditional, Ottoman textiles
Barocco, Kalıcılar Han 31 – master silversmith Aruş Taş's shop; simple, affordable pieces alongside the fabulous, ornate and expensive
Derviş, Keseciler Caddesi 33–35 – good quality rural crafts shop
EthniCon, Tekkeciler Sokak 58–60 – contemporary and highly

fashionable patchwork kilims; fixed prices

Galeri Şirvan, Keseciler Caddessi 55 – respected carpet dealer

Kalendar Carpets, Tekkeciler Sokak 58–60 – good Anatolian carpets from $1,000 upwards; located on main strip for carpets

Kurtoğlu Carpet, Zenneciler Sokak 24–26 – well-designed carpets and rugs

Lumes, Zincirli Han 16 – dazzling Ottoman-style chandeliers

Pako, Kalapakıçılar Caddesi 87 – good handbags and purses

Şişko Osman, Zincirli Han 15 – eponymous shop of the Bazaar's most famous carpet dealer; highest quality

Timur Turistik Eşya, Çukur Han 5, off Yağlıkcılar Caddesi – incredible selection of Central Asian coats and fabrics

Yörük, Kürkçüler Sokak 16 – specialist in ethnic rugs, especially from the Caucausus

BEYOĞLU

İstiklal Caddesi

Beyoğlu's great pedestrianized artery, İstiklal Caddesi, is a vast and very long, glaring parade of storefronts, neon signs and people. The shopping centre of choice for most Istanbullis.

Asya Pazarı – an alley running off İstiklal near glasswear shop Paşabahçe, where you get factory seconds for next to nothing

Beymen, 62 – top Turkish department store

Emgen Optik, 65 – fashionable sunglasses in case you left yours at home

Hacı Bekir, 127 – Hacı Bekir, chief confectioner at Topkapı, was the inventor of *lokum* (Turkish Delight); the business, started in 1777, is still in the family and their produce should banish any lingering bad memories caused by trying Fry's Turkish Delight (a horrible British chocolate bar with a sickly, gooey centre purportedly inspired by Turkish Delight) as a child

Mahmut, 43 – quality, bespoke gentleman's shoes

Mavi Jeans, 117 – top trendy Turkish denim brand, big in the US and comparatively expensive

Nazaryan, 117 – nice footwear for the ladies

Oxxo, 146 – pretty, cheap clothing for younger women

Robinson Crusoe, 389 – excellent English language bookstore, with plenty on Istanbul and Turkey, and a superb fiction selection

Vakko, 123-125 – big name in Turkish fashion, sells range of labels including own-labels

Off İstiklal Caddesi

Butik Katia, Danışman Geçidi 37, Galatasaray – purveyors of the most famous hats in town and family-run since the 1940s; bespoke and ready-to-wear for fashionable women

Homer Kitabevi, Yeni Çarşi Caddesi 28, Galatasaray – excellent bookshop English language academic and current affairs sections; the place to go for books on the politics of Turkey and the Middle East

Ottomania, Sofyalı Sokak 30-2, Azmalımescit – valuable antiquarian Ottoman items; essential for serious collectors

Down the steep hill from the Galatasaray Lycée is Çukurcuma, a once slum-like antiques district currently going through a dramatic rise in fashionability and property prices thanks to the influx of trendy creatives. The area is now an exact equivalent to London's Notting Hill, except in Çukurcuma the antiques and bric-à-brac are more authentic and still affordable. Not for long, though…

Faık Paşa Yokuşu

One of the best roads for browsing and purchasing, though there are great shops scattered throughout Çukurcuma's winding streets.

A La Turca – showroom (and owner's house) full of decorative objects (don't miss the stacks of antique ceramics in the basement)

Accenturc – sculpture, lighting, furniture, painting and jewellery all on show

Anadolu Mezat – Anatolian furniture and designs; most are subtle reproductions

Hakan Ezer – furniture and interior designer, well known for his sophisticated leather

Anadol Antique House, Turnacıbaşı Sokak 55 – wonderfully eclectic collection of curios

Decocom, Çukurcuma Sokak 42 – modern, decorative fabrics made with traditional Anatolian techniques

Leyla, Altıpatlar Sokak 10 – range of antique clothes, fabrics and tapestries

Selden Emre, Çukurcuma Cammii Sokak 31 – reputable and quality antiques and curios dealer

Stoa, Hayriye Caddesi 18 – sculptural furniture from designer/sculptor Tardu Kuman

NİŞANTAŞI AND TEŞVIKIYE

Fashionistas and those for whom the bazaars of the Old City sound like a distasteful nightmare should head straight for the smart residential and commercial districts of Nişantaşı and Teşvikiye, where Istanbul's haute bourgeoisie roam freely.

Abdi İpekçi Caddesi

Abdi İpekçi Street is the closest the city has to Bond Street or Madison Avenue, though it's a good dealer smaller, leafier and nicer than either of those streets. This is where Turkey's up-and-coming designers show off their stuff alongside the usual list of top international brands.

Arzu Kaprol – top Turkish fashion designer with international following

Beymen – newest and classiest branch of top Turkish department store

Cassandra Shoes – fashionable shoes

Decorum – cool modern household objects from international designers and by new Turkish designers, My Name is Eve

Derin Design – custom-made sofas that can be delivered to anywhere in Europe within six weeks

Esas – Swiss–Turkish brand selling everything the stylish young businessman could want: suits, shirts, ties and briefcases

Hakan Yildirim – another top Turkish fashion designer

Nazan Pak and Ela Cindoruk – small and trendy jewellery boutique

Elsewhere in Nişantaşı and Teşvikiye

Ayyıldız, Atıye Sokak 8 – his-and-hers swimwear brand with (just hers) spin-off lingerie range

Gönül Paksoy, Atıye Sokak 6 – unique fashion designs based on contemporary reinterpretations of Ottoman clothes

Sema Paksoy – modern jewellery designer incorporating ancient symbols and motifs; appointment and serious enquiries only on +90 544 520 1207

Zeki, Tunaman Çarşısı, Akkavak Sokak 47 – premier and stylish Turkish swimwear label

play...

There is only one major exception to the Turks' general disregard for sport, be it active participation or passive appreciation – football. Istanbul's three famous teams, Beşiktaş and Galatasaray from the European side, and Fenerbahçe from the Asian, are feared both on and (until fairly recently at least) off the pitch. An Istanbul derby, if you can catch one during the season, which runs from August till May, is a sight (and sound) to behold. The Beşiktaş stadium, which is near the Dolmabahçe, is the most accessible.

Apart from the odd kid trying to maim passing tourists with a football you are unlikely to see much sporting action in Istanbul. Joggers are regarded as dangerously eccentric and gyms are few and far between. There are some pool tables, however (try the bars on Galata Bridge); Istanbul's only dartboard is located at the back of the ground floor of the James Joyce pub. But with the recent increase of major sporting events in Istanbul, the city's first Formula 1 race having followed swiftly on the heels of the hosting of the European Cup Final, sporting options may become more extensive over time.

More joy is to be had on the therapeutic front. Swimming provides a pleasing break from the hustle of the big city. The absolutely stunning pool at the Çırağan Palace or the less chic but trendier pool on Buz Ada, the pontoon-cum-island that floats just off-shore from the stretch of night clubs in Kuruçeşme, are the best options. Sadly, despite having more shoreline than any other city around, the nearest decent beaches to be found are on

the Black Sea coast or on the Marmara Islands, both of which tend to be swamped when it's hot and are about half a day's journey away.

Then there is of course, the *hamam*, or Turkish bath, experience, which involves lying around on heated marble slabs in a large and often beautiful stone room, and, if you wish, being soaped and massaged. Once all Turks visited the baths

and a century ago there were several thousand in Istanbul, but advances in mass-market plumbing and the corrosive effect of fashion have put paid to the *hamam* as a truly popular destination. Now only about a hundred are still going and most of the best known survive on tourist trade, meaning they are relatively expensive and can provide poor service. Pick the wrong *hamam* and you will find yourself going through the tired motions of an ancient ritual – being ripped off. In some, the charade of a wash'n'rub is almost entirely dispensed with; in others the 'masseurs' tread a fine line between massage and physical assault. However, Çağaloğlu and Çemberlitaş *hamams*, both in the old city, are showcases of the aesthetic beauty and atmospheric power of the old *hamams* and the levels of service should be acceptable.

To guarantee more therapeutic results, however, the inauthentic but gentler and more careful *hamam* experiences offered by hotels such as Swissôtel and the Çırağan are recommended. Meanwhile spas, those *arrivistes* of the luxury hygiene scene, have arrived in Istanbul, but when in Rome…

Though a firm second to football, basketball is popular in Turkey. The big three Istanbul football teams have their own teams, as do Efes, the beer manufacturer, and Ülker, which make biscuits. The season runs from October to June. Check websites for details.

Beşiktaş
Tel: 0212 261 6319 www.besiktaskjk.com.tr

Efes
Tel: 0212 665 8647 www.efesbasket.org

Fenerbahçe
Tel: 0216 347 8438 www.fenerbahce.org

Galatasaray
Tel: 0212 574 2916 www.galatasaray.org

Ülker
Tel: 0212 559 4819 www.ulkersport.com

Istanbul is surrounded by water and has more shores than one could wish for, thanks to its borders with the Sea of Marmara, the Golden Horn and the Bosphorus. But if you want a strip of decent sand and unpolluted water you have to go to the Marmara Islands (Marmara and Avşa are the main islands), about two hours away on the high-speed hydrofoil sea buses or six on the standard ferries. An archipelago in the Sea of Marmara, the islands have nice beaches but are a major summer destination for holidaying Turks who can't afford to go elsewhere. So it's best to go either end of the holiday season, from late June to mid-

September. During the season the high-speed hydrofoils leave from Bostancı (10am on) and Yenikapı (10.30am on). Ferries leave from Eminönü (8.30am on). Alternatively see Buz Ada in the Swimming section below.

FAST CARS

Turkey welcomed its first Formula 1 Grand Prix race in August 2005 at the newly built Istanbul Otodrom, which is actually about 60km south of the city on the Asian shore. Check the website of the Turkish Motorsports Organization (www.msoistanbul.com) for details of forthcoming F1 and other car races.

FOOTBALL

Football is *the* Turkish sport, in the sense that the Turks don't really play any others (okay, except for basketball). Still at least they're good at it. Turkey surprised the world, but not themselves (they thought it a travesty that they didn't win), by coming third in the last World Cup. At home domestic rivalry between Istanbul's three main teams is famously fierce. Galatasaray is traditionally the club of the city's upper crust, thanks to the club's historic connection with the elite Galata Lycée, and has recently moved from the infamous and feared Ali Sami Yen stadium to the newly built Atatürk Olimiyat Stadium in Ikitelli. Fenerbahçe, on the Asian side, once the greatest club in Turkey, was Atatürk's and, traditionally, the army's team. Beşiktaş meanwhile, well, they're just Beşiktaş. The football season runs from August-May.

Beşiktaş, İnönü Stadium, Dolmabahçe Caddesi, Beşiktaş
Tel: 0212 236 7202 www.besiktasjk.com.tr

Fenerbahçe, Şükrü Saraçoğlu Stadium, Kadiköy
Tel: 0216 330 8997 www.fenerbache.rg

Galatasaray, Atatürk Olimiyat Stadium, Ikitelli
Tel: 0212 688 0223 www.galatasaray.org

Kemer Golf and Country Club
Tel: 0212 239 7010 www.kg-cc.com

Established in 1995, the swanky Kemer Golf and Country Club is the city's premier country club (without admittedly facing too much competition for the title) and the best place to go if you fancy a round of golf. Located north of the city towards the Belgrad Forest, which borders the Black Sea, it has an 18-hole course, the largest number of tennis courts in Turkey and an equestrian centre. The Club is in the process of finishing a boutique hotel on the grounds, so that if you really enjoy sports that much, you won't have to leave. In the meantime the Çirağan Palace runs special golf holiday packages with the Kemer Club (check www.ciragan-palace.com). Those intending to visit the Kemer Club under their own steam should call ahead to book their day passes.

GYMS

Gyms are rare in Istanbul. If your hotel doesn't have one you haven't got many options.

Flash Gym, 4th Floor, Aznavur Pasajı, İstiklal Caddesi, Beyoğlu
Tel: 0212 249 5347

As long as you don't mind your gyms being basic and working out while you are engulfed in a miasma of sweat then the Flash Gym is for you, being in fact, one of the only options in Beyoğlu. The basic interior décor is complemented by scary-looking but friendly staff. It's about 10 YTL a session.

Marmara Istanbul, Taksim Square
Tel: 0212 251 4696 www.marmara.com.tr

One of best gyms in town has the full panoply of modern gadgetry and equipment, professional instructors, a good view of

Taksim Square and nice aquatic options like a sauna, Jacuzzi and outdoor pool. It's quite pricey at 30 YTL for a day pass.

Early on the Turks perfected the old Roman institution of the steam bath, encouraged by the Islamic belief that physical cleanliness is close to godliness as well by the enjoyment of a good old soak. Like the classic Roman bath, a proper *hamam* has three rooms: the hot room (*caldarium*) for getting all steamed-up and subsequently massaged, the warm room (*tepidarium*) for washing, and the cool room (*frigidarium*) where one could relax a bit before changing and heading to the *camekan* (reception-cum-lounge area). Traditionally the experience didn't stop there for until the infernal 20th century brought modern plumbing to Turkey, the *hamam* was a major social hub, where you would hang out with your mates (same sex of course – men and women frequenting either unisex baths or using the baths at different times) and talk over tea. Thanks to progress everyone now has showers, but can't remember the names of their best friends.

There were more than 2,500 a century ago, but now there are only around a hundred working *hamams* left in Istanbul. Most in the central areas, and certainly those in the Old City, survive almost exclusively on the custom of tourists who are after an authentic Turkish experience. Sadly all that easy tourist money has corrupted many *hamams*, turning them into rip-off joints with (ironically) poor hygiene and lazy masseurs. Others survive in more working-class districts where the baths still have a community function. Don't expect any fashionable and/or wealthy Turks you know to be impressed by your foray into local culture when you tell them about visiting a *hamam*. With little regard for political correctness they regard *hamams* as the preserve of the undesirables (the poor, gays, etc) and tourists. (See below for *hamams* that are in fact gay-friendly.)

Despite all this negativity it's worth visiting a *hamam* at least once, especially those that are architecturally stunning. For all their faults the more touristy ones are at least easy to use.

Expect to pay around 25 YTL for a massage. Each *hamam* has a menu of service options, but in practice that essentially means a choice between DIY or hiring a masseur. Don't be afraid of insisting on better service if you need to. Alternatively, for the hygiene equivalent of Russian Roulette, try going to a non-touristy *hamam* where the menus are only in Turkish and then order at random. Will you get a pedicure or an all-over-body depilation? It's all part of the fun.

Büyük Hamam, Potinclier Sokak 22, Kasımpaşa, Beyoğlu
Tel: 0212 238 9800

The imaginatively titled 'Big Hamam' is one to try if you want a non-touristy *hamam* that is relatively central. Built by Sinan, it might be big but it's still pretty.

Çağaloğlu Hamam, Prof Kazım Gürkan Caddesi 34, Çağaloğlu, Sultanhamet
Tel: 0212 522 2422   www.cagaloguhamami.com.tr

Built in 1741 by Sultan Mahmut I, and untouched since then, the Çağaloğlu Hamam is the city's most famous and one of the most attractive. Ten minutes up the road from the Hagia Sophia, it's brought in tourists for centuries, including, apparently, Tony Curtis, famous for his enjoyment of baths. Though the service can be mediocre, this is a good *hamam* to try.

Çemberlitaş Hamam, Vezirhan Caddesi 8, Çemberlitaş
Tel: 0212 522 7974

Built by Sinan in 1584, the interior is beautiful and atmospheric, which, along with its proximity to the Grand Bazaar, means it's very popular with tourists. Nonetheless it is clean and decent, though make sure you get your money's worth of massage.

Köşk Hamam, Alay Köşkü Caddesi 17, Çağaloğlu, Sultanhamet
Tel: 0212 512 7397

Near the Topkapı, the Köşk Hamam is a small, 15th-century *hamam* that can be hired after hours for families, parties or merely the intensely private (during normal hours it's for men only).

An alternative to the old purpose-built *hamams* and the not especially Turkish spas is to visit the mini-*hamams* run by many of the top hotels as part of their fitness centres. Service is completely personal but more expensive. Try the *hamams* at the Çirağan Palace and Swissôtel.

No *hamams* are officially gay-only, and the managements wouldn't admit it, but the following are well known and popular in the gay community:

Ağa Hamam, Turnacıbaşı Sokak 66, Çukurcuma, Beyoğlu
Tel: 0212 249 5027

Çukurcuma Hamam, Çukurcuma Caddesi 57, Beyoğlu

SPAS

Dreamlands Spa, Küçük Bebek Caddesi 6, Bebek
Tel: 0212 263 8642

Opened in 2003 and inspired by a beach in Bali, Dreamlands Spa brings all those Far Eastern techniques and philosophies together in a menu of massages and treatments. Located outside the city centre it caters primarily for the wealthy locals.

Motus Wellness Club, Abdi Ipekci Caddesi 33, Tesvikiye
Tel: 0212 291 5282 www.motus.com.tr

New, trendy and located in fashionable residential district of Tesvikiye, just north of Beyoğlu, Motus offers a range of treatments, massage and spa treatments as well as yoga and other taught sessions.

Swissôtel Istanbul, Bayıldım Caddesi 2 Maçka
Tel: 0212 326 1100   www.istanbul.swissotel.com

The plush five-star Swissôtel Istanbul has the best spa facilities of the large hotels.

Swimming is about the easiest sporting or pseudo-sporting activity you can do in Istanbul. All the large hotels (Hyatt Regency, Hilton, Carlton, etc) have pools of one sort or another. These, however, are the best:

Buz Bar on Buz Ada, Galatasaray Adasi, Kuruçeşme
Tel: 0212 263 6373   www.buzbar.com

A floating pontoon off the nightclub and bar strip of Kuruçeşme, Buz Ada (*ada* means island) is technically owned by Galatasaray Sports Club. The recent introduction of a swish bar complete with pool has transformed it into a trendy hangout, which is immensely popular during the summer, unsurprisingly given the perverse attractiveness of swimming in, or lounging by, a pool that floats on the Bosphorus.

Çirağan Palace, Çirağan Caddesi 32, Beşiktaş
Tel: 0212 258 3377   www.çirağan-palace.com

The Çirağan Palace's 33-metre-long pool is a spectacular place for a swim, bordering the Bosphorus and separated from it by the thinnest of margins. It is costly, though, at around 80 YTL for a day pass, which means you can also use the Jacuzzis, steam rooms and indoor pool.

Marmara Istanbul, Taksim Square
Tel: 0212 251 4696   www.marmara.com.tr

The outdoor pool at the Marmara Istanbul is pretty small, but for a quick dip and the chance to catch a few rays of sun it's a good option, being so easily accessible in Taksim Square. Its sister hotel, the Marmara Pera, has a stunning rooftop pool, which sadly is reserved for guests. Try sneaking, brazening or bribing your way in for a chance to swim.

info...

Istanbul is a relatively safe city, especially given its size. Some outlying neighbourhoods are slightly more dangerous than the centre. Obviously, do not wave your money around in touristy areas.

Police: 155, Fire: 110, Ambulance: 118

The main ferry docks on the European shore are Eminönü (Sultanahmet side) and Karaköy (Beyoğlu side). From there ferry boats will take you to Üsküdar, Haydarpaşa or Kadiköy (running from north to south) on the Asian shore. Most journeys cost less than £1. Ferries offering a Bosphorus cruise travelling almost to the mouth of the Black Sea leave from Eminönü several times a day, starting at 10am on weekends and 10.30am on weekdays. The full cruise, up and back again, takes 6 hours (just go north to south if pushed for time and take a taxi back).

On 1 January 2005 Turkey got rid of lots of unsightly zeros floating around on its banknotes by replacing the Turkish lira (TL) with the new Turkish lira (YTL). One new Turkish lira is worth a million old Turkish lira. The currency was not revalued or devalued at the time. At the time of writing (summer 2005) the new Turkish lira was worth:
£1 = 2.4 YTL, US$1 = 1.3 YTL, €1 = 1.6 YTL

Key to making yourself understood when attempting Turkish words and names is knowing how to pronounce the language. All Turkish words are spelt phonetically, so it is straightforward. Special Turkish characters, however, are pronounced in the following fashion:
c – 'j' in 'jerry'
ç – 'ch' as in 'cheese'

ğ – silent but elongates the proceeding vowel; so 'Beyoğlu' is pronounced 'Bey-o-loo'

ş – 'sh' and in 'shed'

ö – like the German 'oe' in 'Goethe'

ü – 'oo' – an elongated sound – as in 'boo'

TAXIS

Taxis are plentiful, relatively cheap and metered, which is handy as they are the only practical way to travel any serious distance in the city. Most taxi drivers are perfectly honest but especially in touristy areas you should make sure that the meter (*taksimetre*) is being used. If drivers try to haggle or set a price insist they use the meter. The day rate (the meter should show '*gündüz*', meaning day) is 1.3 YTL minimum, and the night rate ('*gece*', midnight–6am) is 1.8 YTL minimum. Atatürk International Airport is 25km from the Sultanahmet and the journey should cost around 20–25 YTL. It takes 30–45 minutes depending on traffic.

TELEPHONE

To phone Istanbul from abroad dial 00 + 90 (country code) + your number. For the international operator dial 115.

TIPPING

Tipping of 10% is standard and expected in cafés and restaurants, but not necessary in bars or cabs.

TRAMS AND METRO

All exist but frankly you are unlikely to use them. The Metro is in its infancy, with only one line running northwards from Beyoğlu to the suburb of Levant. More usefully the Zeytinburnu–Findikli tram runs along shore of the Sea of Marmara, northeast through the Old City past the Grand Bazaar and along Divan Yolu to Sultanahmet.

index